Praise for

*From Pain to Power*

"*From Pain to Power* is a beautiful book that brings hope to those who have suffered from the darkness and devastation of sexual violation. Author and counselor Mary Ellen Mann does a masterful job in describing survivors as Princess Warriors who have suffered the battle against their royal birth and rightful femininity. I highly recommend this book to survivors of sexual violation and those who love and care for them."

—Boz Tchividjian, executive director of GRACE

"*From Pain to Power* is an informative and compassionate road map for those healing from the trauma of sexual abuse. The Christian perspective of this valuable resource will help many women heal, not just emotionally and physically but spiritually as well. Mary Ellen's vulnerable sharing of her own journey will encourage others toward the restoration and freedom she has found."

—Milan and Kay Yerkovich, authors of *How We Love*
and *How We Love Our Kids*

"Mary Ellen Mann's *From Pain to Power* is an excellent resource for sexual abuse survivors. Told with candor, backed by clinical practice, and full of scriptural insight, this book will help anyone battling back to health after the devastation of rape."

—Mary DeMuth, author of *Not Marked: Finding
Hope and Healing after Sexual Abuse*

"Mary Ellen Mann walks hand in hand with women overcoming sexual trauma. She exposes the lies of the world and reveals the truth God yearns to share with us—we are more precious than silver, more costly than gold, and more beautiful than diamonds. *From Pain to Power* journeys through the effects of sexual violation and leads to the reclamation of every woman's worth as beloved daughters of God."

> —SHANNON ETHRIDGE, relationship coach, speaker, and
> author of numerous books including the million-copy,
> best-selling Every Woman's Battle series

"Mary Ellen Mann has brilliantly taken a painful and often confusing topic and offered a solid path to move forward—beyond the scars and heartache. In a powerful weave of truth and reflection, she teaches readers how to not only understand abuse and pain but to aggressively fight against it. This is a 'go-to' book for years to come."

> —GARI MEACHAM, president of Truly Fed Ministries and
> The Vine Uganda, speaker, and author of *Truly Fed:*
> *Finding Freedom from Disordered Eating, Spirit*
> *Hunger,* and *Watershed Moments*

"In my twenty-three years as a journalist, I've encountered all kinds of cases of abuse and objectification. Mary Ellen has written a guide not only for those who've been victimized but for all of us. *From Pain to Power* is a step-by-step journey of self love, faith, and understanding. It speaks to anyone grappling with doubt and beautifully elevates those who have spent too long blaming the wrong person: themselves."

> —BROOKE WAGNER, anchor of *Good Day Colorado*

"*From Pain to Power* validates and gives hope that healing, love, and joy are possible after the humiliation and degradation of sexual violation."

—MARILYN VAN DERBUR, advocate, speaker, and author
of *Miss America by Day*

"This powerful book truly validates victims of sexual trauma while empowering them to walk with God, using spirituality as a tool; also a helpful resource for therapists working with sexual trauma victims."

—ROOPA KURSE, MD; adult, child, and adolescent
psychiatrist

"You are a hero! Read this book and you will be able to look in the mirror like a Navy Seal who says 'I will never quit.' Mary Ellen is personal, informative, and loving as she champions you to be a warrior in your story and to know that you are a gift from God. Read this book and the impact, growth, and change in you will be recognizable."

—JOHN E. DAVIS, MA, author of *Extreme Pursuit,*
president and founder of 2xtreme

"Mary Ellen Mann uses her personal narrative and engrossing story to provide clear strategies for transformation. As a therapist who has seen men and women struggle with sexual violations for more than twenty-five years, I would recommend *From Pain to Power* to every church leader, counselor, and Christian parent."

—JOHN DEVRIES, executive director of development at
Shelterwood Academy

"What a powerful resource for sexual abuse survivors and those who care about them! Drawing from her own personal and professional experiences, as well as from her deep faith and heart of compassion, Mary Ellen Mann takes the reader on a hope-filled journey—from the dark tunnel of pain and trauma, onto paths of insight and truth, and ultimately to the high places of redemption and healing. You, or someone you love, can be whole again—this book will show you how."

—SANDI BANKS, author of *Anchors of Hope*

"*From Pain to Power* is a must-read for women across the globe who bear the tumult of sexual violation. We must recognize the sacred value of survivors of abuse, while acknowledging and encouraging the power of their voices. This book is a great tool for those who work with survivors to help them stay the course in their healing. You, too, can step into her journey and help her reclaim her life as you learn to restore her value and purpose."

—KIMBA LANGAS, executive director of Free the Girls

"*From Pain to Power* is a journey into the battle wounds and resulting scars of a survivor of sexual violation. You are also given a road map to help women find healing and wholeness again. Read this book to be part of the solution to this epidemic concern."

—DALE INGRAHAM, co-founder of Speaking Truth in
Love Ministries, president of MK Safety Net, and
pastor in Campbell, NY

# from PAIN
## to
# POWER

MARY ELLEN MANN, LCSW, MS

*from* PAIN
*to*
POWER

OVERCOMING SEXUAL TRAUMA
*and* RECLAIMING YOUR TRUE IDENTITY

WATERBROOK
PRESS

FROM PAIN TO POWER
PUBLISHED BY WATERBROOK PRESS
12265 Oracle Boulevard, Suite 200
Colorado Springs, Colorado 80921

Trade Paperback ISBN 978-1-60142-772-4
eBook ISBN 978-1-60142-773-1

Published in the United States by WaterBrook Multnomah, an imprint of the Crown Publishing Group, a division of Penguin Random House LLC, New York.

WATERBROOK and its deer colophon are registered trademarks of Penguin Random House LLC.

Library of Congress Cataloging-in-Publication Data
Mann, Mary Ellen.
    From pain to power : overcoming sexual trauma and reclaiming your true identity / Mary Ellen Mann, LCSW, MS.—First Edition.
        pages cm
    Includes bibliographical references.
    ISBN 978-1-60142-772-4—ISBN 978-1-60142-773-1 (electronic) 1. Christian women— Religious life. 2. Sexual abuse victims—Religious life. 3. Self-perception in women. 4. Self-perception—Religious aspects—Christianity. I. Title.
    BV4527.M255 2015
    248.8'6—dc23
                                        2015022504

Printed in the United States of America
2015—First Edition

10 9 8 7 6 5 4 3 2 1

SPECIAL SALES
Most WaterBrook Multnomah books are available at special quantity discounts when purchased in bulk by corporations, organizations, and special-interest groups. Custom imprinting or excerpting can also be done to fit special needs. For information, please e-mail SpecialMarkets @WaterBrookMultnomah.com or call 1-800-603-7051.

*To my sister, Kathleen. Princess Warrior, you are filled with the glory of the Trinity. Semper fi.*

Then your light will break forth like the dawn,
    and your healing will quickly appear;
      then your righteousness will go before you,
    and the glory of the LORD will be your rear guard.

                      —Isaiah 58:8

But for you who revere my name, the sun of
righteousness will rise with healing in its rays.
And you will go out and frolic like well-fed calves.
Then you will trample on the wicked; they will be
ashes under the soles of your feet.

                      —Malachi 4:2–3

So do not fear, for I am with you;
    do not be dismayed, for I am your God.
      I will strengthen you and help you;
    I will uphold you with my righteous right hand.

                      —Isaiah 41:10

He will cover you with His feathers,
    and under His wings you will find refuge;
      his faithfulness will be your shield and
      rampart.

                      —Psalm 91:4

# Contents

# Publisher's Note

# Acknowledgments

High praise is owed to those of you who have moved me forward when I could have collapsed, when I thought I was failing. You have known more confidently than I that my story and insights could play a part in the healing of others.

Special mention goes to those who have loved me through the awkward process of gluing the pieces of my broken trust into one whole person. I have been healed by your patience, passion, kindness, and enduring loyalty. Maybe you wrote me a card; baked me a cake; reached out to me through an e-mail, a text, or a call; or hugged me when I wanted to run away from this project. Some of you, remarkably, called on me to help you.

My husband has withstood the most wretched parts of my coming together. Through it all you saw my present beauty—ashes, blood, and all. You have shown me Jesus in your consistent, unflinching presence, as if the terror simply provided an opportunity to display the power of devoted, courageous love.

My heart is forever indebted to my children, whose innocent love has covered the many open wounds with a salve I never knew was available. Your pictures and cards of encouragement adorn the walls of my bedroom and closet because they are the high art of God, showing me what wholeness looks like. You have known how my abundant affection can mix too often with my strange anxieties, and you have loved me patiently and sweetly despite it. God gave me your tender lives to show me what I could have never known I had in my heart—unmitigated, unrestrained love. God protect and make happy your golden lives.

My sister, every day you rise out of the ashes of severe emotional pain. You do this to fight for your future, your hope, and your children. You reach toward me, no matter how bloody your wounds, to make sure I know you are here for me. Hour after hour, whether late night or early morning, you have read through this book to offer insight and stability. Deep canyons of loneliness and fear have been filled by your friendship and reassurance. Gratitude and love to you forever for all you have given to this effort and for all that you represent.

I thank all Princess Warriors for your bravery and valor to overcome the lies perpetrated in the violation you suffered. You are unsung heroes for generations to come—never doubt that. Your lives are the nutrients in the soil of this effort. More importantly, I hope that as you find your story on these pages, you understand—confidently—how much I adore you, enjoy you, and respect you.

Ron Lee, my editor—you met me in my despair at a writer's conference in April 2014. By a stroke of mercy, you decided this project was worthy. You fought for this manuscript in meetings I'll never know about. You were my *hosanna* in the furnace of doubt and nearly giving up. Plucking me out of obscurity was a huge risk. Words will never do justice to describe my gratitude. Deep gratitude and prayers for total success as you venture into your new endeavors.

Susan Tjaden, when Ron needed to pass the baton, you cared with kindness, warmth, vision, and concern. Thank you for holding me up in the final details of this process in the early and late hours—when no professional should be working. Your approachable depth and wisdom energized and encouraged me more than you'll ever know. Your team, with Kim Von Fange, was unbelievably helpful. I don't know what I would have done without you.

To everyone at WaterBrook, your eye for design and layout and the careful copyediting (even doing statistics for me!) has been validation I didn't know I was missing. In the work you've done, you have captured something far more exquisite than I could have imagined. For those of you working on marketing and publicity, I felt your strength and kindness in the first e-mails. Thank you for carrying this work into the hands of those who deserve care and leadership as they gather their strength to work against the ravages of sexual trauma. You all have helped this worthy population of women know that they are created to thrive in power and hope, reclaiming their true identity.

Indeed, you live out one of my favorite quotes:

We are each other's harvest;
We are each other's business;
We are each other's magnitude and bond.
                    —Gwendolyn Brooks

I am forever indebted and utterly grateful.

*Introduction*

# YOUR PERSONAL INVITATION

I invite you to join me and others in reclaiming things we fear we have lost: purpose, vision, personal value, and power, among others. The journey will build, starting from a place of having faced sexual violation in its many forms. It will continue on to deal with the ways that violation has affected us. And finally, we will reclaim ourselves, our lives, our power, and our worth as daughters of God.

I am a trained therapist, having worked in private practice for more than fifteen years. Much of my practice involves working with girls and women who struggle with who they are following episodes of sexual trauma. We work together, using the best practices developed from years of experience with women who have overcome the effects of violation.

I also work with clients at a very personal level. For more than twenty-five years, starting at an early age, I had to deal with the trauma of being the target of inappropriate sexual behavior. As I write this book, and as you and I journey together, I represent a fellow overcomer.

Together, we will start from where we are today. We will move toward living out the legacy God has given to us by his Spirit and through his Son, Jesus Christ.

## FACING THE WORLD WE LIVE IN

In God's eyes you are royalty, a daughter of the King. Nothing can change that, but the systems of the world seek to destroy what God has named you, and me, and all of his daughters. We have to hear and trust what he says to us. God looks at us and says, "You are beloved. You are more valuable than anything you can imagine. You are my daughter, and nothing will ever change that." That is a glimpse of what is true about you.

However, sexual violation is a weapon that brings harm, attacking all that God says about you. Beyond the trauma of being targeted, there is the fallout that we have to face afterward. We will address these questions one by one in the chapters that follow. You already know them well:

- Am I a bad person who deserved this?
- Did I somehow invite this?
- Was I singled out due to a flaw in my character, or my lack of faith, or some other personal weakness?
- If I didn't deserve this, why am I so destroyed by it?
- Why did violation come at the hands of someone I trusted: a family member, friend, boyfriend, teacher, husband, coach, or church leader?
- Will I ever reclaim the person I used to be?
- How can I protect myself from ever having to go through this again?
- How can I regain the power I feel was taken from me?
- What does it mean to be royalty, a daughter of God, when I have been the target of violation?

You know already that the work will not be easy, but we will labor together to find the answers to these questions and others. You can live in the reality that you are more valuable in God's eyes than all other things. You can live the life that God wants for you, regardless of what happened in the past. You can learn new habits of living and thinking; you can practice new ways of being. And by the end of the journey, you will have grown in insight, understanding, identity, and power. You will regain who you are, and the wisdom you acquire will help reset your life.

We will walk through your past, opening doors in your memory where you were sexualized and brutalized. Know that Jesus goes there with you, and I will be there as well. We will turn on the lights in every room, and we will work through the issues until every scared and lonely place is restored.

God, through Jesus, redeems what has been broken. God will restore to you what has been taken, and you will be made whole. You will get your real girl back—whether that girl is social or quiet, whimsical or analytical, artistic or scientific. There is so much more *for* you and so much more *about* you beyond the trauma in your past.

## REJECTING BLAME

No matter where you are today, know this: The violation was not your fault. No matter what the person told you or accused you of. No matter if you didn't fight him, if you never told anyone, or if someone implied that you invited overtures due to your looks, manner, or way of dress. Sexual violation is *never* a woman's fault.

You are made by holy and respectful Hands, the Hands of a holy and respectful Father. Your life is fully known by your Father. He knows you to be unique, unmatched, the first and last of your kind.

You survived sexual violation. That is one true fact about you. But it is not a fact that identifies you. Yes, you are a Princess Warrior who bears scars from past battles. You know the piercing of wounds against your femininity. But what *identifies* you is the unchanging truth that you are the daughter of the King of kings. You are a member of the royal family of God. You are worth more to your Father than you can ever imagine.

Those are things that define you for eternity. They will never change; they always will be true about who you are. Meanwhile, there are other things that describe details of your past. They don't describe you, but they do recall what has happened to you. For instance, you were singled out for sexual violation. That doesn't mean that you are alone in this, but it does mean that many women around you were not targeted at that time. Why you?

We will explore that question in a later chapter. For now, know that you are part of a huge number of girls and women who have suffered something similar. As many as one in four females alive today has been the target of some form of sexual violation.

If you have talked about this in the past, it is possible that you were not believed. Or perhaps the person you talked to tried to minimize your experience: "It couldn't have been as bad as you're saying. He must not have meant it. Maybe you did something to send the wrong signal. Even if it did happen, you need to forgive it, forget it, and move on."

Accusations and false assumptions don't apply here. You need to know that I believe you, and together we will explore the whys. We *will* get to the other side of this.

Marilyn Van Derbur wrote a memoir, *Miss America by Day,* about her recovery from thirteen years of incest committed by her father. She wrote about a confrontation in which she revealed to her mother just a small portion of what she had suffered. Her mother turned away from her and said,

> "All I want is peace. I will do anything for peace." That did it. I found myself doubling my fist and ramming it into the table as I rose to my full height and raged, "That's what got us here in the first place. You were willing to do anything for peace. Don't rock the boat. Don't open the door. Don't raise your voice. *Sometimes you have to go to war to have peace, Mother.* Sometimes you have to stand right up to someone and cry out, *'No more. Stop!'* Sometimes there's fighting and bleeding in order to have peace."[1]

You might identify with Van Derbur's experience. Many of us do. Along with one in four women who have faced similar trauma, I stand with you. God, your Father, stands with you. He will walk beside you as you experience his restoration of your life. Those who do not look away, those who stand with you and fight for you, are the new family and friends who matter most.

Reading a book like this can be daunting, maybe even a bit lonely and embarrassing. But remember, one of every four women you know, meet, or interact with has endured sexual trauma. You are very much *not* alone.

## TRUTH FROM GOD THAT EXPRESSES
## WHO YOU REALLY ARE

Ask God to open your eyes and heart so you can start seeing yourself as God sees you. Scripture provides sweet truths that identify how the Father, the Son, and the Holy Spirit care for you, what they see when they look at you, and who you are as an adopted coheir to the throne with Christ. Ponder these truths from Scripture, and meditate on them until you are convinced they describe you as God sees you.

Because I, [insert your name here], am in Christ, I am *secure*.

- I am a child of God (see John 1:12).
- I am free forever from condemnation (see Romans 8:1).
- I am assured that in all things God will work for my good (see Romans 8:28–29).
- I am free from any condemning charges against me (see Romans 8:33).
- I cannot be separated from the love of Christ (see Romans 8:35).
- I have been established, anointed, and sealed by God (see 2 Corinthians 1:21–22).
- I have been given the Holy Spirit as a pledge guaranteeing my inheritance to come (see Ephesians 1:13–14).
- I can do all things through Christ who strengthens me (see Philippians 4:13).
- I have been rescued from the dominion of darkness and brought into the kingdom of Christ (see Colossians 1:13).
- I am hidden with Christ in God (see Colossians 3:3).

- I have not been given a spirit of timidity but of power, love, and self-discipline (see 2 Timothy 1:7).
- I am born of God, and the evil one cannot touch me (see 1 John 5:18).

Because I, [insert your name here], am in Christ, I am *significant.*

- I am the salt of the earth (see Matthew 5:13).
- I am the light of the world (see Matthew 5:14).
- I am God's child (see John 1:12).
- I have been chosen to bear fruit that will last (see John 15:16).
- I am Christ's personal witness (see Acts 1:8).
- I am God's temple (see 1 Corinthians 3:16).
- I am a part of Christ's body (see 1 Corinthians 12:27).
- I am a minister of reconciliation for God (see 2 Corinthians 5:18).
- I am God's fellow worker (see 2 Corinthians 6:1).
- I am a saint (see Ephesians 1:1).
- I have been raised up and am now seated with Christ in the heavenly realms (see Ephesians 2:6).
- I am a citizen of heaven (see Philippians 3:20).

Because I, [insert your name here], am in Christ, I am *accepted.*

- I am Christ's friend (see John 15:15).
- I have been justified (see Romans 5:1).
- I am united to the Lord, and I am one with him in spirit (see 1 Corinthians 6:17).
- I have been bought with a price and belong to God (see 1 Corinthians 6:20).
- I am a member of Christ's body (see 1 Corinthians 12:27).

- I have become righteous (see 2 Corinthians 5:21).
- I have been adopted as God's child (see Ephesians 1:5).
- I have direct access to the Father through the Spirit (see Ephesians 2:18).
- Since I am God's daughter and because God sent the Spirit of his Son into my heart, I can call out, "Abba, Father." I am no longer a slave, but God's child; and since I am his child, God has made me also an heir (see Galatians 4:6–7).
- I am invited to approach God with freedom and confidence (see Ephesians 3:12).
- I have been redeemed and am forgiven of all my sins (see Colossians 1:14).
- I am complete in Christ (see Colossians 2:10).

God placed his Spirit into your life not to give you restraints and fear, but to give you power, love, and a sound mind (see 2 Timothy 1:7). Like a loving parent, the Triune God wants you to integrate his power, love, and sound mind into *your body*.

May the Lord bring miracles of insight, strength, protection, and promise to you. Let the victorious Savior, the Lord Jesus Christ, meet you here. Say to him out loud: "Meet me here. Show me you are here. Show me you know me. Show me as soon as possible. Give me the senses to detect you. Amen."

As we move forward together, I want you to claim this truth about yourself: you are anointed for a special purpose only you can fulfill—a purpose that can be further defined by your battle scars.

## Chapter 1

# I HAVE WALKED
# WHERE YOU WALK

Because most of us have been persuaded to see sexual violation as *our* secret, many of us may remain silent, revealing it (if ever) only to a select few. But shame grows in silence. My dream is that it becomes commonplace to discuss this reality rather than hiding it.

It is only fair that I let you know about my experiences. I have braided my own story throughout this book to remind you that you are not alone. I recovered my voice, and you can too.

For thirty years, I normalized my brokenness. Since I denied the destruction in my life, I never asked God to glue me together. Breaches of trust had become routine to me, where being lost, lonely, and scared was simply life as I knew it.

I had been led to believe that love was about sex, sexiness, and physical attraction, starting when I was only five years old. Threaded into countless conversations were dirty jokes, ongoing sexualized commentaries on my body and looks, abuses of power through solicitation for emotional comfort, and inappropriate touch that ranged from long full-frontal hugs to uncomfortable kisses on the mouth. In my childhood, the violations were paired with verbal and physical abuse.

Because of a lot of influences in my early life, I believed I was responsible for everyone. I was a compassionate person by God's design, so I became a perfect target for outlandish boundary violations. I was voted "most gullible" in high school, not an award I was proud of. I was bullied at a Christian elementary school for being a snob because my family had a large income and a fancy address. To avoid the bullying, I started spending recess in the classroom to avoid everyone. I felt responsible for everyone's interpretation of me.

My body developed early. Of course, I had no choice in the matter. If I could have unzipped myself from my body and traded it for a thin, undeveloped one, I would have. My home life was filled with running commentary that often involved sexual innuendo and critical accusation. I was told lewd things and given feel-up hugs. But if I gained any weight or looked in any way less than I "should have," I was told my face and arms were looking "too full" and to close the refrigerator door.

When I attended a Christian junior high, I was well liked by some girls in my grade, but I was constantly sexualized by boys. They would rate my quickly developing body during lunch. They would make up songs and chants about sexual favors I should do for them. Because of this attention, I was hated by the girls in eighth grade. The girls would scream across the field during breaks, "We hate you, 44DD!" One girl lit into me about my bra size. Her tirade lasted the entire bus ride from the junior high to the elementary school, where we were dropped off.

The day I was chastised on the school bus, I cried and ate a box of chocolate thin mints. One of my parents saw the wrappers and said, "You can't do this kind of eating, so just get over it." My heart started to seal up in sugar and silence. This began my binge eating and over-exercise routine for the next fifteen years.

While still in junior high, all the girls were ogled by the high-school boys. Word got out that a senior student thought I was an attractive eighth grader. When I entered high school as a freshman, I was targeted by older girls who made me clean up their lunch trash. Girls on the yearbook staff put unattractive candid pictures of me in the school annual. Since I never considered myself anything but mediocre at best, I felt utterly confused by the attacks.

## THE FALLOUT

While I have never been raped, the crimes against me were psycho-emotional, subtle, and slimy physical moments that left me feeling that the enemy was *me*. I couldn't escape the feeling that I was deeply flawed. The evidence was that by nearly everyone I looked up to and nearly everywhere I went, I was sexualized and humiliated. Added to this was the abandonment of people who were supposed to protect and lead me. I was alone, rejected, ridiculed, and made the target of inappropriate sexual comments and advances.

I felt that my path was littered with insurmountable obstacles, and I was motivated by dread and fear. Dread and fear gave me a deep energy to avoid the truth of my broken heart. In high school, my soul sought protection inside a stone battlement.

I gave up trying to feel any expectation, thought, or need. As I rejected normal thoughts and feelings, I was energized by terror and a never-ending cycle of self-loathing. I loathed myself because I perceived that what I was experiencing was my fault, my weakness. My only "victory" was maintaining perfection—just a thin, crusty layer of external perfection. I added in high grades, extreme activity, and busyness. I tried to soothe the abiding terror with compulsive secretive overeating, compulsive overexercise, and starvation.

I had no protective boundaries. Men continued to take shots at me, and they found their mark. I was repeatedly injured by words, inappropriate touch, meanness, and the invasion of privacy. As I grew more and more devastated, I resorted more and more to hiding. Along with that came a loss of appetite and suicidal depression.

In addition, there was grabbing, groping, and voyeurism, especially when I was in high school and college. Such breaches occurred at the hands of those I once trusted as Christian leaders, friends, and family members.

Once I left home at age eighteen, I endured still more years of sexual harassment, stalking, and emotionally incestuous disclosures by those in authority. These things were done by church and youth-group leaders, college professors, and men in leadership in my work environment. Meanwhile, my family fell apart in the wake of a scandal, and my first marriage crumbled under verbal and emotional abuse.

While nearly all the unwanted attention came from men who claimed either to be Christian and/or were part of my family and social system, some of the childhood violation occurred at the hands of older girls who also were in my family and social system.

Back then, I doubted that what happened really mattered, rationalizing that "it could have been so much worse." Yet if you looked at my anxiety and inability to really trust that *I* was safe, that *love* was safe, you would see the cancer created by my just-survive mind-set.

When I became a therapist, I did so reluctantly. I had been to a lot of therapy, and it didn't really seem to help. When I attended graduate school, I planned to work in lobbying and policy—that's where "real" change took place, I believed. But it turned out I wasn't meant to go that route. Through a series of events, I backed into a primary-therapist position and then stumbled into a private counseling practice that continued to grow. I kept thinking, *I'll just do this therapy thing until my policy job comes along.*

After nearly three years of working as a therapist, it hit me. The counseling I had undergone hadn't helped because I never talked about my sexual violation. I kept shelving it.

But until I could talk about it and be loved in the midst of it, all the pain would be woven into my present life. My self-doubt, self-criticism, and distrust of everyone around me would continue to sicken me psychologically and spiritually.

My experience of recovery was filled with tension, wariness, and loneliness. I was tense with the pressure of threat and dread that had worked itself into every cell in my body. I was wary of whether I should place my wounded expectations into the hands of another. I was deeply lonely, believing I made people do these things to me because they had happened in every segment of my life, year after year. The repetition of the sexual violation taught me that it was *my* shame and, thus, it was *my* problem to bear alone.

Although the details of my story are sure to differ from yours, perhaps you will relate to the ways my personality and view of God had formed like scar tissue around my injuries. I will weave throughout this book my process of distinguishing God's *truth* for who he designed me to be from the *fiction* of what the violations had tried to convince me I was.

I want you to know that I resonate and empathize with you because I am a therapist. But far more than that, I walk with you as a restored and redeemed Princess Warrior—a woman who has waged battle against the assault on her life, a woman fighting against the forces that have persuaded both you and me to question hope, security, and our sense of meaning.

You are a princess because you are made by the King of kings, Jesus Christ. He formed you and knew you before you were born. And he died to offer you a way into his royal family. Through Jesus's victory over death, you are under grace and can cry out, "Abba, Father" (Romans 8:15). You are made a coheir to the throne of Christ (see verse 17). By choosing Jesus, you inherit his royal identity.

You are a princess, and you are a warrior. On this side of heaven, we women are too often devoured for our beauty and influence. We are subjugated by insults and assaults. According to the United Nations Development Fund for Women report in 2013, one in three women across the globe will be sexually assaulted in her lifetime.[1] We have sixty million survivors of childhood sexual abuse in the United States alone, according to ParentsforMegansLaw.org.[2]

And rape is the fastest-growing violent crime in the United States.[3] Annually, rape costs the country more than any other crime, $127 billion.[4]

The worst part is that this act of violation overwhelmingly occurs at the hands of people either in the family or integrated into the family social system. In fact, 34.2 percent of children who are sexually abused are abused by family members, and 58.7 percent are sexually abused by someone known to the family.[5]

It is a battle to break free from sexual trauma, and we will prepare for that battle. Though the original plan for humanity was not to live under siege, it is indeed the case today.

Sexual violation creates a riptide in the soul because one's fundamental capacity to trust her body and her instincts is stolen from her. To have the lines of dignity crossed in the psychological and sexual realm is an event that stuns the nervous system. A person's sense of confidence twists into questions: "Am I real?" or "Am I okay?" We feel broken and silenced. While there are differences among us, such as how intense the violation was, the trauma registers the same in your mind and in every organ and system within you.

## LEARNING THAT GOD IS NOT FRAGILE

God can handle all of our pain, our anger, our confusion, and our brokenness. He won't be put off by repeated questions or desperate pleas for help. He is not fragile; he won't lose patience and start tuning out our requests. His willingness to listen and to respond will not run out.

I had to learn to trust God. It involved not trying to appease him but instead telling him what I really needed. My unconscious mind kept lying to me: *God is fragile and will shatter if you upset him.* I had been treating God like I learned to operate with everyone around me. *Be careful not to upset anyone, and everyone will care about you,* I reasoned.

I knew Christ died for me, but I didn't know he really *enjoyed* me or *wanted* me in his family as his coheir, as a daughter of the Father. Not only was God not fragile, but he was willing to lose everything to be on the hunt for me—his lost, lonely sheep.

I let God know I wasn't protecting him anymore from what I really thought, felt, and needed. I wanted God to be my Defender—

strong and resilient—or I didn't want God at all. I needed proof that he was who he claimed to be, and eventually I became a believer again.

## WHAT CREATED YOUR BATTLE SCARS?

When we hear the term *sexual violation,* we may think of something extremely violent that would show up on the evening news. If you endured sexual trauma that involved less violence, you might conclude that the violation was of less consequence. I used to tell myself, *It could have been so much worse,* and so do the countless women I meet. In my counseling practice, I hear all sorts of minimizations: "He only touched my breasts, so it wasn't a big deal." "My stepdad was always gross. At least it wasn't my dad or someone related to me." "It happened so long ago, and he wasn't mean about it."

If we refuse to look at our experiences squarely, our injuries can slowly infect our thinking and expectations, thus influencing our habits and choices.

When an injured athlete starts to compensate for unhealed injuries, what started as a knee problem, for example, can evolve into a back and neck issue. The athlete's pain spreads to other joints, just as it does in the personality of the Princess Warrior. On the other hand, when the athlete takes the injury seriously and seeks immediate help, the protocol of physical therapy or even surgery will keep the injury localized and health will be regained more quickly.

If you try to minimize the injury of sexual violation, it is likely to spread to other areas of your life. But take the story of your sexual violation seriously, seek help, and understand that a team of people are normally needed to help bring healing, and you are likely to navigate through the distress without it controlling your choices and attitude in the future.

I join Oprah's indignation about minimizing sexual abuse based on the severity of the physical acts:

> What really upsets me and what you don't seem to get, America, is there aren't varying degrees of abuse. It's about the abuse of power and trust. So whether you physically penetrate a child with your penis or your finger or an object, whether you *just* touch their breasts, whether you *just* fondle them or you *just* kiss them, it doesn't matter. It's an issue of trust and power. . . . America doesn't understand that it is the raping of the spirit and the soul.[6]

Any breach of trust that involved unwanted sexual advances, especially when the aggressor has more power over you, is a *raping of the spirit and the soul*. Since any unwanted sexual encounter constitutes abuse, I urge you not to minimize what happened.

Dr. Dan Allender provides a good description of what constitutes sexual abuse in his book *The Wounded Heart*. Take a deep breath, and ask yourself if anything below speaks to an experience you had at any age.

- Sexual abuse is any contact or interaction (visual, verbal, or psychological) between a child/adolescent and an adult when the child/adolescent is being used for the sexual stimulation of the perpetrator or any other person.
- Sexual abuse may be committed by a person under the age of eighteen when that person is either significantly older

than the victim or when the perpetrator is in a position of power or control over the victimized child/adolescent. When the sexual abuse is perpetrated by an adult or older child who is a blood or legal relative, it constitutes incest, or intrafamilial sexual abuse. Sexually abusive words produce the same damage as sexually abusive contact.

*Types of Sexual Abuse: Contact and Interaction*

- **Contact**—genital intercourse; oral or anal sex; unclothed genital contact, including manual touching or penetration; unclothed breast contact; simulated intercourse; sexual kissing; sexual touching of buttocks, thighs, legs, or clothed breasts or genitals

- **Interactions**

    *Verbal*—direct solicitation for sexual purposes; seductive (subtle) solicitation or innuendo; description of sexual practices; repeated use of sexual language and terms

    *Visual*—exposure to or use of pornography; intentional (repeated) exposure to sexual acts, sexual organs, and/or sexually provocative attire (bra, nighties, slip, underwear); inappropriate attention (scrutiny) directed toward body (clothed or unclothed) or clothing for purpose of sexual stimulation

    *Psychological*—physical/sexual boundary violation: intrusive interest in menstruation, clothing, pubic development; repeated use of enemas; sexual/relational boundary violation: intrusive interest in child's sexual activity, use of child as a spouse surrogate (confidant, intimate companion, protector, or counselor)[7]

These definitions point out the wide range of behaviors, words, actions, and inferences that, singly and together, constitute sexual abuse. It is not helpful to say a child was "*only* exposed to pornography" but not sexually touched. The mind-body connection hardly sees the difference. There is no good, better, or best in terms of how the trauma plays out. It isn't what was done to you; it's how it makes you feel. The effect of the abuse has the deeper power and hooks the individual into beliefs and behaviors that increase his or her sense of pain and insignificance.

Sexual harassment can have elements of touching and nontouching, as Allender points out. Princess Warriors who are hurt "only" through sexual harassment have no reason to feel they are not engaged in the battle at the same level as another daughter of God who was raped. Those who have been stalked and sexually harassed need a legion of people to bring hope and comfort, to rise on their behalf and cover them in sympathy and advocacy.

Some of you who are reading this book are being sexually violated in your marriages. You may have been cheated on, and while it was not a violation against your body personally, it is an enormous betrayal. If something has happened to you that makes you doubt that sexuality is safe, you have been hurt in this way.[8]

## SCAR TISSUE

The deeper the injury, the more severe the scar tissue. Sexual violation leaves us injured, and one of the hardest aspects of restoration is not caving in to the injuries. We have to exercise and do the equivalent of physical therapy to make sure scar tissue doesn't develop.

In later chapters, I will share in greater detail my personal journey with sexual harassment and the touching and nontouching violation I endured. In many ways, being targeted for purposes of stalking and sexual harassment was like grabbing a snake by the tail. I couldn't keep the serpent far enough away to avoid repeated bites and injury. It would take years to understand how the messages from previous violation influenced my ongoing unrest, nightmares, severe anxiety, social withdrawal, nihilistic thinking, and insidious distrust of everyone around me.

My journey of restoration began with a person in authority who finally took me seriously and, unlike others, believed me. I mention this because none of us can do the work of healing and being restored alone. You and I need others who show us they can be trusted, and we need helpers with expertise in a variety of areas to come alongside us in the healing journey. To assist your restoration, I want you to know I stand with you. I don't promise a quick or easy solution, but I do commit to helping straighten out the question marks that surround you. I want to help rebuild your confidence, your sense of personal worth, and a clear view of the power you possess as a daughter of God.

You can awaken from the numbness that follows violation. You can be reintroduced to God and his desire to bring about your regeneration. He wants to restore you to the person he made you to be. (It is understandable, if not expected, that you may vacillate in your confidence in God. That is an area we will look at during the journey.)

Having gone through my own dread of trusting someone to care about me and having witnessed the doubt and faith cycles of my family, friends, and clients, I know it is natural to question and doubt. You are invited to think, feel, and express to God what you are really going through. No one here will judge you, and God will not disown one of his children.

Later in the book we will work through concepts, homework, prayers, guided imagery for picturing Christ's healing, and other practical measures you can use to honor and grow into the person God made you to be. Keep your questions close while you open your mind and heart in the safety and privacy of your reading. Be who you are, doubts and all.

Let's step into this together, just one foot in front of the other. My daily prayer is that God richly and abundantly blesses you with his restorative comfort and provision.

## Chapter 2

# THE WARRIOR'S POWER
# AND ROYAL DESIGN

But you are a chosen people, a royal
priesthood, a holy nation, God's special
possession, that you may declare the
praises of him who called you out of
darkness into his wonderful light.

—1 PETER 2:9

We declare God's wisdom, a mystery
that has been hidden and that God
destined for our glory before time began.

—1 CORINTHIANS 2:7

Princess Warriors, you have been attacked because of your beauty,
your strength, and your threat to the Enemy, who wants you weakened, alone, and silenced. This might seem counterintuitive, but think
about it. Satan is committed to trying to silence those whose lives and
words bear testimony to the love and power of God (see Revelation
17:6). In their best-selling book *Captivating: Unveiling the Mystery of*

*a Woman's Soul,* Stasi and John Eldredge describe a spiritual war being declared on women:

> [The Evil One] hates Eve.
>
> Because she is captivating, uniquely glorious, and he cannot be. She is the incarnation of the Beauty of God. More than anything else in all creation, she embodies the glory of God. She allures the world to God. He [the Evil One] hates it with a jealousy we can only imagine.
>
> And there is more. The Evil One also hates Eve because she gives life. Women give birth, not men. Women nourish life. And they also bring life into the world soulfully, relationally, spiritually—in everything they touch. Satan was a murderer from the beginning (John 8:44). He brings death. His is a kingdom of death. Ritual sacrifices, genocide, the Holocaust, abortion—those are his ideas. And thus Eve is his greatest human threat, for she brings life. She is a lifesaver and a life giver. Eve means "life" or "life producer." . . .
>
> Put those two things together—that Eve incarnates the Beauty of God *and* she gives life to the world. Satan's bitter heart cannot bear it. He assaults her with a special hatred. History removes any doubt about this. Do you begin to see it?[1]

As a woman, you are a life giver. And even more, you embody the beauty of God. That makes you a formidable figure in opposition to the Enemy, who does nothing but evil in the world. The Eldredges write about the effect of Satan's opposition on women: "Most of you thought the things that have happened to you were somehow *your fault*—that you deserved it. If only you had been prettier or smarter or done more or pleased them, somehow it wouldn't have happened. You would have been loved. They wouldn't have hurt you."[2]

Don't buy those lies.

Satan opposes God by hurting all that God has made, every bit of creation. Satan starts with Eve, who is known as the finest and most complex of God's work. Eve is a life-maker and is emblematic of God's supreme intelligence, fine features, stamina in the face of pain, and deep capacity for sacrifice. A woman has a soulful courage to expose her heart as a mother, caretaker, and friend. My counseling practice is visited by women who walk into the fire as they enter my office, craving a solution and courageously fortifying themselves against the lies of Satan. His lies come through the mouths and actions of those who have oppressed my counseling clients.

The God of justice is on your side. As part of the bride of Christ, you and I and all daughters of God stand in glory. But Satan does not want us to know this truth. We stand in battle to restore our true identity, as Psalm 46 declares:

> God is our refuge and strength,
>     an ever-present help in trouble.
> Therefore we will not fear, though the earth give way
>     and the mountains fall into the heart of the sea,
> though its waters roar and foam
>     and the mountains quake with their surging. . . .
>
> God is within her, she will not fall;
>     God will help her at break of day.[3]

## A WORD ABOUT MEN

To be clear, I am not against men. While men have wounded me, they have healed me in ways only a man can. I am a mother of two boys and a wife to one of the most golden men I know. On countless nights my husband has read Scripture to help me fall asleep after I awaken in the middle of a spiritual attack. He searches for the light and leads me through prayers that help me contend against the darkness. (I will offer these prayers in a later chapter.) My husband has the courage to support my work.

My family of men has healed me. I praise God for this and wouldn't have it any other way. I know they are soldiers for God.

Boys and men stand just as vulnerably as girls in this world. Boys are deeply wounded by the same people they love and need. I have met and read about countless men who are even more silently reeling from the effects of their pain, both in the way society has told them to manage their pain and in the way they turn their pain on others.

In fact, sexual trauma against a boy or young man can be perceived as even more intractable than sexual trauma against a girl or young woman. This is because the popular image of "true masculinity" assumes that no such trauma exists. When it happens to a male, his masculinity is questioned by his subculture, if not his entire culture, and his wounds are rarely addressed. A male survivor needs rehabilitation and advocacy as much as a female survivor.

However, we will focus more on female survivors. This is because theirs is a much larger population. According to reports provided by the National Center for Juvenile Justice, "Females were more than six times as likely as males to be the victims of sexual assault. . . . More specifically, 86 percent of all victims of sexual assault were female. Nearly all forcible rapes (99 percent) involved a female victim."[4] According to the US Department of Justice's National Crime Survey, it was calculated that 346,830 American women were raped in 2012.[5]

The crime of sexual assault, while frequently committed by men, is perpetrated by women as well. Some of you experienced sexual abuse at the hands of a woman. Please know that the traumatic impact is no less than what takes place at the hands of a man. One client told me that she thinks it's more ostracizing to be victimized by a woman. All of which makes the experience of those who are targets of sexual abuse by women even more wrenching. I ask your forgiveness in advance if I do not adequately cover the female perpetrator by mainly using masculine pronouns. Please know that you have my attention as I write about perpetrators of either sex.

I often say that a sign above the entrance to my counseling office should read "For the brave and mighty only." Women who come seeking healing leave behind the image of a quiet, accepting woman. They are now ready to wade into the maelstrom of anger and doubt. They are here to talk through the messy emotions that receive no compliments but which must be processed.

They no longer cling to an "acceptable" image, worshiping instead no one but the Lord who carries them through this gritty—and often devastating—loss of ideals and false hopes. Too many outsiders (family members, pastors, friends, even some therapists) want to truncate the anger of a Princess Warrior. It leaves us depressed, addicted, compulsive, and very, very alone. Speak up and speak out. If others are uncomfortable with your honesty, so be it.

As you muster the courage to enter this process, know now that you are set apart for greatness. Paul affirmed you even as he sent a warning to Christians living in ancient Ephesus: "For our struggle is not against flesh and blood, but against . . . the spiritual forces of evil in the heavenly realms" (Ephesians 6:12). Satan is real, and he is intent on destroying everyone he can. He destroys some as he influences them to damage others in acts of sexual violation. And in doing that, Satan attacks daughters of God who are damaged by predators.

Princess Warriors know that their courage comes forth in the face of challenge and loss.

In later chapters, we will look squarely at the profound evil you endured. I want you to feel safe enough to hate what has happened. You have an advocate and a friend in me, and also in the friendship of the Holy Spirit. The Spirit of God wants to speak to you as you rage with your doubt and questions, and as you search for the purpose of it all.

Dostoevsky wrote, *"My hosanna has passed through a great furnace of doubts."*[6] A survivor of sexual trauma will experience total defeat and will doubt God's goodness. Logic will demand that you sort all this out until a reason becomes clear. Why were you singled out for abuse? Why did someone who should have loved and protected you instead decide to abuse you? Why didn't someone protect you from abuse? Logic insists there must be answers to such questions; meanwhile, it wars against a faith-based acceptance of not knowing why.

It is your right to doubt a lot of things. That is part of the process, but don't allow the hard parts to obscure the destination. When you finish reading this book, I want you to never have to wonder again whether your pain deserves to be healed in safety and compassion.

I want you to know, without question, that you are whole and unique to God.

## LIVE IN THE TRUTH ABOUT YOURSELF

I encourage you to live in the depth of the knowledge that you are formed in love and that you have the right to protect yourself and all that you value. Think of your life as a castle, with walls, gates, a moat, and a drawbridge. It is yours to claim with soulful worship of God, who will—in his truth and mercy—help you to erect and fortify your boundaries.

God wants your castle to be secure and protected, yet open to others. God wants you to look out for yourself, much like a good parent teaches her child assertiveness, voice, awareness of her gut instinct, and even methods for fighting back.

We will talk more about this in a later chapter. For now, though, know that God already has defined who you are. We will explore who he says you are and then work toward accepting your true identity.

We will then move to ways to engage the healing process on a spiritual, psychological, social, and physical level. This is where we begin to practice the inside-out method of becoming a Princess Warrior.

We will work through proven techniques that will help train your heart and mind. You need to feel and think of yourself in light of the truth, in the same way that God sees you and delights in you. Beyond your thinking, you can adopt practices that have been shown to develop your ability to stand up for yourself.

You, a Princess Warrior, are created to overcome violation and to feel the pleasure of healing. God shaped the course of the planets, and he made you to be who you are. He created the capacity to bring justice to the oppressed. He has committed his creation to a purpose of greatness to shape eternity. Every tear and every wound holds exponential power. Every moment of terror and insignificance holds shining justice and eternal, mind-blowing change—change that alters everything forever. *You* will change things forever. Yes, *you*.

People can be hurt by people, and they can be healed by people. You will get to know a community of those who will help care for you, to assist in your recovery.

We wage a battle against terror, shame, and contempt that others often cannot understand. We battle the vast inner landscape of our self-doubt and our doubts about God's goodness. We stand up to the deep whisper that says it was our fault: "I should have stopped it . . . I should have fought harder . . . I should have told someone . . . I must have deserved it . . ." Standing up, speaking up, fighting against the lies and indignity of sexual violation—in whatever form it happened to you—that is what we will do before the last chapter of this book ends.

Our Designer alone has the capacity to touch the emotional leprosy of our abuse and make it a new place of power, hope, truth, creativity, passion, compassion, laughter, inspiration, leadership, and victory.

"It is close at hand—a day of darkness and gloom, a day of clouds and blackness. Like dawn spreading across the mountains a large and mighty army comes, such as never was in ancient times nor ever will be in ages to come" (Joel 2:1–2). You are in that army, and so am I. We fight a battle along with countless others.[7]

"It is for freedom that Christ has set us free" (Galatians 5:1). We are free to love, to know, to stand, and to feel deeply. You are free to rise to the opportunity to speak love, hope, and joy into your own life.

## Chapter 3

# IF GOD IS ALL-POWERFUL, WHY WERE YOU ABUSED?

> The crags of doubt and the valleys of despair
> offer a proving ground of God that no other
> terrain can provide.
>
> —DAN ALLENDER, PhD

A great source of grief for many or perhaps most Princess Warriors is that God does not choose to relieve our pain expediently or in the way we expect. With that reality before us, is there anyone who still wonders why we struggle with doubt?

You and I are at war with an entity that is godless and empty of life. It preys on you and your life like a parasite. Satan doesn't want you dead, and he doesn't want you alive. He wants you in the middle: lifeless, uncentered, dispassionate, and confused. This way you have no energy to invest in transcending mediocrity. Signs of this would be half-finished pursuits, unrequited passion, lack of focus and direction, and the inability to gain vision and follow where it leads.

There are arguments that postulate that evil is the absence of God, just as cold is the absence of heat and darkness is the absence of light. If I choose to avoid incorporating Christ into my experience or choices, I am not admitting that he doesn't exist. I am using my free will to cut myself off from his activity and power. I am cutting off Christ's heat and light. Light overcomes darkness by virtue of physics, not subjective interpretation. Thus it stands to reason that God's light overcomes darkness. And darkness, or evil—for instance, in the reality of sexual violation—is the absence of God. Further, the act of sexually violating another person is a choice made in/by their own free will. It is an attempt to destroy another.

Evil exists in God's absence, and it comes into being when human beings abandon the choice to do what is right. But why doesn't God simply get rid of free will and thereby protect all of us from making self-destructive decisions and from harming others? In response to that question, apologetics scholars typically answer that God wants a relationship with us based on desire. Rick Warren, author of *The Purpose Driven Life,* further explains that "God wanted a race of tested individuals who choose to love him, and you can't love someone unless you have a choice not to love him. As soon as love is forced, it's not love anymore."[1]

One of my clients was a victim of sexual abuse committed by a female baby-sitter. My client had been raised by an alcoholic mother and an emotionally absent father. Her home life led to painful experiences. I asked her how she reconciles evil with a loving God, and she said, "I would rather have the choice to love and live according to who I am made to be, than be protected from evil. God has given me a choice to move through this pain and triumph. I would rather have choice than be free from pain." This woman is a mother of four now and is learning to live beyond her trauma.

Another contested issue is that love should rescue us from all pain. This perhaps is the deepest wound I have experienced personally. If there is power in love (and I believe there is), why doesn't it help relieve the unbearable pain? This raises a deep trust issue with respect to God. If God loves me, why does he not rescue me from the lingering effects of violation? And, to get straight to the point, where was God when I was being victimized for twenty-eight years by a series of men who had influence and power on their side? Why did God allow such evil to enter my world, and yours?

The answer that is true and that possesses the power to ultimately rescue us is this: evil is loose in the world because of the fallen nature of humanity—all of humanity. Don't try to pinpoint behaviors or thoughts on your part that might have led to your being abused. Such an exercise is not helpful and is bound to frustrate you. First of all, you did not invite abuse, ever. And second, the abuse had nothing to do with your sin on a personal level. It had everything to do with the sin of humanity, shared by everyone who has ever lived.

Because sin brings the consequences of evil, which act against us, God released his Son into this world to save us. That is the only answer to the problem of evil that helps us heal.

I often use the following analogy: If a drunk driver hits my car, does that mean God is punishing me for choosing to drive? Or was I a bad driver and, because of that, I got hit? Was it a freak accident, a matter of happenstance? I have yet to hear a drunk driver admit to targeting a particular motorist before causing a collision.

So why do we treat sexual violation as if the perpetrator spent a lot of time choosing one particular victim? And why do we accept the accusations that we are somehow responsible, that we are not smart enough, or careful enough, or good enough to avoid attracting the attention of predators?

The sin of sexual violation against another is like that of drunk driving. There is no objective and no identifiable purpose in a predator's choice of a target. It's like the freak accident of getting hit by a drunk driver. The violator commits the crime in desperation and unfocused evil. Just as a drunk driver chooses to drink and then drive, so does a perpetrator choose to commit a destructive act. It is clear that acts of sin leave behind casualties.

Rather than focus too much attention on evil, let's recall God's role in saving us from the outcome of evil that exists on earth. To preserve our free will and remain true to his own nature, God provided atonement for evil through his Son, the Lord Jesus Christ. Jesus proved that God's love exercises power over all evil. Jesus gives us his Spirit, the Holy Spirit, which makes every one of us an overcomer (see John 16:33).

I am not saying that the atoning work of Jesus puts an end to acts of evil in this world or that it instantly removes the pain of sexual trauma. But the saving work of Jesus is the power of God to save us from being controlled by the way other people treated us. There is great benefit to us beyond eternal life in God's presence after we die. The atoning work of Christ bestows power, wisdom, insight, and guidance in our lives as we struggle with the effects of sin on earth. Let's look at what the Bible says about the impact of God's love on each of us in our daily lives.

## THE PROOF OF GOD'S LOVE AND CARE

The Bible is not an ordinary book; it is a living text. Each time I read it, something new is born in me. God's Word gives me a new pair of eyes and then yet another when I return to it later.

The New Testament reveals the salvation story, showing God's love and grace at work on our behalf, and making clear the cost of our salvation through the life, death, and resurrection of the Lord Jesus Christ. He displays the attributes of God himself in his unlimited power, total knowledge, and ever-present, unchanging, and eternal nature. His miracles called attention to the truth that God's kingdom is coming (see Isaiah 35:5–6). It is also by Christ's authority that sins are forgiven.

As a Princess Warrior, I understand that my fellow overcomers might struggle to trust God. Good news here: Our Father is fine with that. He just wants engagement, even if your engagement at the moment is shouting at him in anger.

God engaged with us first when he decided to make us in his image. Because we bear the image of God, it follows that we are fully expected to engage him in questions and doubt and anger as well as in trust and praise. We see in Isaiah 1:18 (ESV) that God was upset with his people, the Israelites, yet he encouraged them to "come [and] reason together" with him. He issued this open invitation to come and talk, even in their disobedience. Everything you need and every burden you carry matters to God. Go to him and begin to talk it out.

Doubt can originate in anger, and anger means you're alive and thinking and feeling. Anger is the emotion we feel in reaction to having been violated. This often is referred to as the fight-or-flight response.

While we were not designed to live in fear, we have a capacity to be self-protective and angry when threatened. It is more than permissible to be bold with God, telling him exactly what you are thinking, feeling, wondering about, and angry about.

The important thing to keep in mind is that we are not owed an answer from God, as Job learned in the Old Testament. In being bold in his presence, we are not putting ourselves above him and telling him he has to explain things. Rather, we turn to God in boldness because he is all we have left.

A healthy sense of self registers violation. We know right away when there is a breach. As we become whole, we will detect *possible* violation; we will be more self-preserving and honoring to our instincts. As people coming to our senses, we feel the problem and the anger. God has designed us to register this emotion so that we act and speak on our own behalf.

Most importantly, though, I ask you to be willing to open the door to your soul. When your trust has been betrayed and when you feel that you are the lowest priority in the eyes of others, you learn that others are not likely to step forward to defend you. That is another reason why we are on this journey together. I fight for you to believe, and I will give you as much room as you need. I fight to provide a place for you to organically grow your faith as you doubt and as you put your hurt and agony before God. I pray you will trust the process enough to recognize and honor the Princess Warrior you have always been.

# Chapter 4

# THIS IS WHERE *You* TAKE CHARGE

The injury [of trauma] is real. The injury is physical. It is not mere confusion or misdirected thinking, or sign of a weak character. It most certainly is not a case of "just get over it."

—SETHANNE HOWARD, MD, AND MARK W. CRANDALL, MD

Demons smell human brokenness like sharks smell blood in the water, and they move in to take advantage of the weakened soul.

—JOHN AND STASI ELDREDGE

After knowing and working with thousands of women in my personal and professional life, I will say with confidence that Satan wounds us where we are most gifted. He wants the Princess Warrior to lose effectiveness in God's work due to her getting lost in the forest of her pain. Satan wants you and me to feel that we have been abandoned. He wants us to lose hope that we will ever be ransomed and redeemed.

Satan wounds many a Princess Warrior by leading her to think

she is stupid, even when her academic record and many accomplishments show just the opposite to be true. He tempts Princess Warriors
who are gifted in organizing, building, and creating to feel scattered
and overwhelmed. I have seen Satan convince respectable and giving
people that they are disliked, unwanted, and inferior.

Again and again, I have seen this type of thing play out. And it
affects women across all classes, cultures, and creeds. A woman of
great physical beauty will be targeted. Afterward, the trauma of sexual
violation will work to convince her that she is unworthy, ugly, and,
most of all, forgettable. My artist clients who are injured by sexual violation often are driven to silence and withdrawal, giving in to the pain
and letting go of their independent voice and creativity. They now
believe they are insignificant.

The injury wrought by sexual violation was not your choice, *but
recovery is.* Survivors of sexual violation tend to live inside the mistaken belief that someone will realize we are feeling trapped, that although we remain silent, someone will arrive to help. That is not what
will happen. You are fighting for your health, your wholeness, and
your life. You have to stand up for yourself. You must restore to yourself what was taken without permission.

Christiane Northrup, MD, author of *Women's Bodies, Women's
Wisdom,* shines a medical light on this truth:

> It is not stress itself that creates immune system problems. It is,
> rather, the perception that the stress is inescapable—that there
> is nothing a person can do to prevent . . . it. . . . If we don't
> work through our emotional distress, we set ourselves up for
> the physical distress. . . .

The uterus has memories, the heart has memories and the skin has memories. *The mind can no longer be thought of as being confined to the brain or to the intellect; it exists in every cell of our bodies.* Every thought we think has a biochemical equivalent. Every emotion we feel has a biochemical equivalent. . . . When [a part of your body] talks to you, through pain or [another manifestation], are you prepared to listen to it?[1]

Until we honor and give voice to those parts of ourselves that lived through the trauma, we will continue to manifest symptoms of our violation. (I will discuss this in greater detail in a later chapter.) For now, however, know that you are embarking on a journey to integrate the truth that defies the lies of the trauma. Truth is a powerful weapon. It can overwhelm the lies that attempt to keep you silent, feeling insignificant, and powerless.

For now, realize that the feelings your body and your mind are sending are not betrayals; they are your nerve endings coming together again. Sometimes there is intense anger, followed by exhaustion and possibly relief. Sometimes there is no feeling, and life seems okay due to its absence. Then, perhaps while you watch a movie or even a commercial on television, a new set of emotions will emerge. It could be a wave of pain, or need, or revulsion.

The wounds of sexual violation carve deception into the thinking of a Princess Warrior, and Satan will come at you where you are strong and/or where you are gifted. He will attack you in that area in an attempt to keep you inactive and isolated. Satan focused on wounding me in the area of significance. I never felt I had anything to offer to anyone or in any situation, ever. To this day I continue to fight that battle against lies such as "No one will care" and "No one needs or wants what you have to offer." It's important to call such reasoning what it is: a lie. But in addition to the lies, you also have to deal with false accusations: "You're a fake and a phony, and no one will believe you."

Keep reminding yourself that the lies and accusations come from Satan. His is the voice that tears down and discredits. His voice attacks and attempts to cut you off from comfort and strength. I remain scarred from the lies I have defended myself against, some of them coming from people who barely knew me and even from those whom I thought had my best interests at heart. It's easy to assume you are the source of your own condemnation. But with insight and discernment, you can see accurately that you face an enemy who wants to remain invisible. Satan wants you to believe that his deception originates within you.

## CONFRONTING SATAN'S CORE LIE ABOUT YOU

Throughout countless interviews with clients, as well as information gleaned from books and medical articles, I have found that the central evil message of sexual violation, especially when it happens at a young age, is this: "This is because of you. This is what you deserve."

Remember, you present a threat to Satan's work on earth. Because you are a very real threat to his evil, he has targeted you. Satan hates that you are the glory of creation, a beautiful Princess Warrior who attracts positive attention. He hates that you are incandescent and the one who makes creation sigh with appreciation for beauty and goodness.

Satan is bent on destruction, and frequently he targets those who are young. Infants and children are frequent targets because the earlier you injure a child, the more intractable and longstanding will be the symptoms of trauma. In those instances, the healing process is lengthier and more involved.

The attacks don't stop with Satan. People often deepen the pain with their unwanted and inaccurate comments. I heard someone say that children are "stupid" because they believe the perpetrator's threats. However, nothing could be further from the truth. It is known that children are concrete thinkers and do not arrive at abstract reasoning until, at the earliest, ten years of age. In their concrete-thinking stage, they engage in black-and-white reasoning. They sponge up information, language, and experiences as true and acceptable, regardless of how evil the acts against them may be. Jesus alluded to this when he described the wrath he wished upon those who cause a little one to sin (see Matthew 18:6; Mark 9:42; Luke 17:2).

God designed children to develop their knowledge and instincts in a healthy and safe environment. But if a child is wounded by sexual violation, she or he will act out in ways that reflect the damage of the shame and insidious assumptions that it was ever their fault. The child who is sexually violated assumes, *This is happening to me because I made it happen.* Thus children struggle to recognize that sexual abuse is abnormal. It is not a natural part of life, nor is it something they caused to happen. And if the abuse came at the hands of someone the child knows, loves, and trusts, she or he will struggle to understand that abuse and incest are forms of predatory violence and that help is both available and necessary.

Children also fear the consequences of reporting. They fear that no one will believe them, they are terrified by how people will react, and they are concerned that the perpetrator will punish them for having told. The primary reason that the public is not sufficiently aware of child sexual abuse as a problem is that 73 percent of child victims do not tell anyone about the abuse for at least a year. Forty-five percent of victims do not tell anyone for at least five years. Some never disclose.[2]

## PTSD IN CHILDREN AND ADOLESCENTS

Children and adolescents who have suffered sexual violation may experience symptoms of posttraumatic stress disorder. Signs include fear of being separated from a parent; loss of previously acquired skills (such as toilet training); sudden issues with stuttering, sleep problems, and nightmares without recognizable content; somber, compulsive play in which themes or aspects of the trauma are repeated; and drawing and writing of sexual or frightening images, such as demonic images with blood- and death-oriented themes. The child may develop new phobias and anxieties that may seem unrelated to the trauma (such as a fear of monsters, sharks, bears, being in the bathroom alone, or going to bed without additional security needs first being met).

They also may suffer physical pains and illnesses with no apparent cause, such as irritable bowel syndrome, eczema, migraines, extremely painful menstrual cramps, insomnia, and asthma. Self-injury can also be a sign of having been abused. It may involve burning, cutting, and pulling hair (including eyebrows, eyelashes, and the hair on arms, legs, and head).

Physical signs can include pain during urination and bowel movements; there may also be pain, discoloration, bleeding, or discharge in the genitals, anus, or mouth.

Children or adolescents may provide clues that seem likely to provoke a discussion about sexual issues. They also may exhibit a sudden change in eating habits, refuse to eat, or have trouble swallowing. In adolescents, you may see compulsive eating or dieting. The child or adolescent suddenly may have money, toys, or other possessions for no apparent reason. A child or adolescent might comment that her body is repulsive, dirty, or bad. Along with displaying problematic eating, she may neglect personal hygiene. She may also start to exhibit adult-like sexual, flirtatious, or seductive behaviors. The child or adolescent may show increased irritability or aggression toward siblings, animals, or peers, or she may ask peers to behave sexually or play sexual games.

Any one sign does not mean that a child has been sexually abused, but the presence of several suggests that you should begin asking questions and consider seeking help. Similar or identical signs and symptoms could relate to other stressors, such as parents in divorce proceedings, the death of a family member or pet, problems at school or with friends, severe losses of property, a car accident, medical trauma, or other anxiety-producing events.

## LONG-TERM EMOTIONAL EFFECTS
## OF SEXUAL VIOLATION

When a child is abused outside the family, the family is likely to support the child. But when the abuser is in the family, the family will struggle to provide the same kind of support and security. I personally understand the way a house is divided: relatives stop speaking to one another, and no one wants to visibly choose sides. But this type of problem isn't a matter of opinion; it's a matter of whether someone will choose to accept evil and abuse. Surprisingly, many do. They often believe it is not a choice but accept it as the status quo. However, it is a choice that often leads to brutal rejection of the survivor. If the parent who is not abusing the child learns of the other parent's abuse and does not stop it—or if the nonabusing parent blames the child for the abuse—this often can be more devastating than the violation itself. Indeed, rather than healing beginning immediately and lasting for only a small amount of time, the healing can take decades.

If the people who are supposed to protect children are causing the abuse, a child's ability to trust is nearly destroyed. Incest survivors typically suffer difficulties with developing trusting relationships. Even in cases of rape in the military, female soldiers report the fracture that occurs is similar to incest because the soldiers are family to one another regardless of rank.

I have learned through my training that, in many cases, the recovery from being raped and even tortured by someone you don't know can be less difficult than being sexually harmed—even if it's less violently—by someone you do know. This list gives examples of the implications of sexual violation for anyone at any age who has been violated by anyone, whether the abuser is in, near, or removed from her circle of trust.

People who are sexually violated may

- blame themselves for the abuse
- have trouble trusting themselves

- feel hopeless or have an ongoing sense of dread or doom
- feel disconnected from others or from life
- fear and avoid healthy affection
- feel betrayed by their bodies
- feel like others don't really know them, or feel that they are living in a reality not shared by others or that is not experienced by anyone else
- feel like they never will really be "okay"
- have physical illnesses and body sensations that feel traumatizing
- feel extremely powerless
- feel a loss of relationship with their parents and family
- live in constant secrecy
- feel angry, even hostile, toward others and themselves
- doubt their ability to accurately perceive reality
- forget or deny everyday experiences
- feel tremendous personal shame
- hate themselves
- learn to abandon their personal safety in dangerous situations
- fear being in relationships, even casual friendships
- have memories, pictures, and sounds that play in their minds and renew the trauma
- feel fearful even during times that are "safe"
- startle easily
- have nightmares or fear going to sleep
- feel abandoned by their parents or other adults

- lose hope in the goodness of humanity
- have a core feeling that they have lost their relationship with God or that they are unloved by God
- doubt that they are worthy of love

## SYMPTOMS AND COPING STYLES IN ADULTS

If they fail to find healing for their anger, doubt, and loss of faith, Princess Warriors may choose instead to rely on destructive coping mechanisms. Here are several long-lasting physical symptoms and relational implications that are associated with sexual victimization.

- Survivors of sexual abuse have more physical health problems than the unabused. These include chronic pelvic pain, extreme premenstrual syndrome, gastrointestinal disorders, and other chronic pain disorders, including headaches, migraines, back pain, and facial pain.[3]
- Notably, 70 to 80 percent of sexual-assault survivors report excessive drug and alcohol use, and they are more likely than the unabused to smoke cigarettes, overeat, and drink alcohol. Further, they are unlikely to use seat belts.[4]
- Young girls who are sexually abused are more likely to develop eating disorders during adolescence.[5]
- Major depressive disorder, generalized anxiety disorder, and obsessive-compulsive disorder are commonly seen among victims of sexual abuse.[6]
- Survivors of child sexual abuse are more likely than the unabused to be sexually promiscuous.[7]

- More than 60 percent of first pregnancies among teenage girls are preceded by experiences of molestation, rape, or attempted rape. The average age of the offenders is twenty-seven years old.[8]
- Both males and females who have been sexually abused are more likely than those who have not been abused to engage in prostitution.[9]
- Breastfeeding can be interrupted by flashbacks triggered by past abuse. Confidence in bonding with a newborn can also be a trigger for women who survived childhood sexual abuse.[10]

Having looked at the leading signs that someone has been violated, as well as the leading symptoms following violation, we will turn now to ways to address the pain.

## Chapter 5

# YOU ARE MADE BY GOD, AND YOUR LIFE IS SACRED

Above all else, guard your heart,
   for it is the wellspring of life.

—PROVERBS 4:23, NIV 1984

The LORD will surely comfort [her]
   and will look with compassion on all her ruins;
he will make her deserts like Eden,
   her wastelands like the garden of the LORD.

—ISAIAH 51:3

As Princess Warriors, we are born with a unique identity and individuality. However, through boundary violations of any kind, especially sexual violations, we can lose our sense of "I." When we lose a clear sense of our identity, we are losing touch with the biblical truth that we are "fearfully and wonderfully made" (Psalm 139:14).

God wants you to live in power. This power is articulated by determining who you are, what you are, and why and how you will live. God wants your devotion so that you can rise to the challenges of life.

Your life is like a sacred castle that Satan tries to attack, so you need fortifications such as strong walls, gates with drawbridges, and moats, because the castle inside the walls is more precious than a museum piece. You and I are living and sacred artifacts, each of us totally unique in all of history.

A Princess Warrior should see that her life is a living organism that grows through repair, renovation, and cleaning. You decide what needs to be cultivated, mended, or renewed. You decide what happens in your being—inside the grounds of your castle. The Spirit of God gives you power, and you were born with free will, the ability to choose and decide. "For God has not given us a spirit of fear and timidity, but of power, love, and self-discipline," Paul wrote to Timothy (2 Timothy 1:7, NLT).

As you make decisions and choices, you can devise a security system to protect yourself against the invasion of evil (see 1 Peter 5:8). The beginning point is to steel yourself to defeat Satan. You can't compromise with him or try to accommodate his overtures in any way.

## FORTIFY THE BOUNDARY LINES

In my early twenties, as I came to terms with the misery of my life, new heartbreak set in. I had been betrayed, but the worst was realizing I had betrayed myself. As a way to operate under threat, I had developed a sympathetic drawbridge for those who did not see my worth or meaning to allow them access to my castle grounds. However, my sympathy toward those who took advantage of my compassion and sympathy ultimately manipulated me. Thus, my originally intact castle began to suffer the ravages of multiple attacks by the Enemy.

Attacks came from many directions, including trusted family members; a Christian-college professor; my first husband, who was a Christian; a Christian counselor; Christian youth-group leaders; Christian bosses and managers where I worked; and even a few of my most trusted Christian friends. No wonder I began to believe the lies of Satan that I was deserving of unwanted sexualizing attention, humiliations, manipulation, and domination. And because I kept attracting (at least it seemed that I was doing the attracting) unhealthy attention from so many Christian men in so many different settings, I thought God somehow ordained my private torment. To clarify, I thought the repetition of these events was a message from God that I was flawed and unworthy of protection, decency, and honor.

We may look at our lives with hopeless and helpless thoughts. Satan will lie to us, saying the ruin is so significant and the repair so involved that it is too difficult to even try. A Princess Warrior can combat the lies and live in the truth. It's a battle, but we are about to gather the weapons we need to silence the lies. First, we will fortify the boundary lines with two basic questions: *What are my rights?* and *What are my needs?*

## WHAT ARE YOUR RIGHTS?

I give nearly all my clients a copy of the Personal Bill of Rights, a list of assertions that spell out their rights to lives that are free of interference, abuse, trauma, and insecurity:

I have the right to ask for what I want.

I have the right to say "no" to requests or demands.

I have the right to state my feelings and needs.

I have the right to change my mind.

I have the right to make mistakes and learn from them.

I have the right to follow my own values and standards.

I have the right to say "no" to anything when I feel I am not ready, or it is unsafe, or it violates my values.

I have the right to determine my own priorities.

I have the right not to be responsible for others' behavior, choices, feelings, or problems.

I have the right to expect honesty from others.

I have the right to be angry at someone I love.

I have the right to be uniquely myself.

I have the right to feel scared and to say, "I'm afraid."

I have the right to say, "I don't know."

I have the right to not give excuses or reasons for my choices.

I have the right to make decisions based on my feelings.

I have the right to my own needs for personal space and time.

I have the right to be playful and lighthearted.

I have the right to be healthier than those around me.

I have the right to be in a nonabusive environment.

I have the right to make friends and be comfortable around people.

I have the right to change and grow.

I have the right to have my needs and wants accepted by others.

I have the right to be treated with dignity and honor.

I have the right to be happy.

I have the right to be loved and supported.[1]

After considering the rights listed above, get out a pen and make your own list. View it as a living document to be revised and updated as you grow personally. If it helps, place notepads all over the house to record new rights or edit existing ones. As you commit to this exercise, you will begin to feel what it's like for your individual voice to emerge.

### Don't Forsake Your Rights

Some of my Christian counseling clients often balk at the idea that they are authorized by God to embrace a list of rights. Many Christians have learned that the good news of the gospel derives from the fact that sinners somehow forced God into coming up with Plan B, after things broke down in the Garden of Eden. After the fall of humanity, a new plan was needed to save us from ourselves. Included in that interpretation is the idea that we can never trust ourselves.

Many of my clients have told me that talk of personal boundaries signifies a lack of faith. Self-expression and personal desire, they believe, are evidence of impulsivity. Being bold in life, they feel, violates the orderly system of obedience and long suffering we are to adhere to.

For too many people, the gospel is understood to be a fear-based message. We are sinners who deserve a fate worse than death. Due to our state of abject worthlessness, Christ took pity on us and died a brutal death. There is no emphasis on God's attributes of love, grace, and mercy or on the fact that God pursues us tirelessly until we choose to come home to him. Instead, we are taught the gospel in negative terms, with all of humanity being the rightfully guilty party.

How does this apply to victims of abuse who have been taught the gospel? They hear: "God resentfully offered up his Son, sacrificed him, and did all of this to make us 'intolerable people' tolerable." I suffered abuse starting when I was a child. Because of that, this explanation of the gospel (God had to hand over his Son to a horrible death, and all because of me) never seemed to be good news. It felt more like tragic news that reinforced the worst things I feared to be true of myself. *Mary Ellen, you are bad and unlovely, and because you screwed up so badly, God is going to have to give up his precious Son. Jesus, while undeserving of any of this, was scourged and crucified because you are so sinful. This is yet more evidence that you are not valuable nor wanted by your family and friends. If you think about it, you aren't really wanted by God either. He just pities you.*

Such a slant on the teaching of the gospel twisted the knife that already was lodged in my shameful, lonely heart.

You might be nodding in agreement, or at least in acknowledgment. You also might struggle with God's love and grace, because the way you were taught the gospel simply heaped more shame and sadness on your head.

I finally understood that I was wanted. I learned that it grieves God to be without me. Like a hen with her chicks, God wanted to keep me from a dangerous end (see Psalm 63:7). He is as holy as he is loving. He has already gone to the greatest length—the sacrifice of his own Son—to restore me to my royal design. The sin I was born into and the sin I participated in was compassionately knocked away from me so that I could be shielded by God and kept safe from the ravages of darkness for eternity. However, God's tender devotion—displayed in his Son's sacrifice—did not become real for me for years.

Many of my clients filter the gospel message through their shame and emptiness, which makes foreign the truth that God longs to be with them. His greatest desire is that they be restored to their places in his family, to shine in the world as God's daughters. God didn't create duplicates when he made each one of us. He created only first-issue originals. He wants you to be strong, opinionated, whole, and willing to explore and live according to your instincts. John Eldredge nails the struggle that we face when battling the "sinner identity" talk. It is nothing less than a shame-based conversion technique that scares people into "making a decision for Christ" and promising to change. It leads to believers quickly escaping a relationship with Christ when the going gets tough.

Eldredge wrote:

> All this groveling and self-deprecation done by Christians is often just shame masquerading as humility. Shame says, "I am nothing to look at. I'm not capable of goodness." Humility says, "I bear a glory for sure, but it is a *reflected* glory. A grace given to me." Your story does not begin with sin. It begins with a glory bestowed upon you by God. It does not start in Genesis 3; it starts in Genesis 1. First things first, as they say.[2]

This sojourn into the good news of the gospel has helped me to be patient with my Christian clients' resistance. Also, when I ask clients whether they would want their children, grandchildren, nieces, or nephews to know these rights listed in the Personal Bill of Rights, they say "yes" without hesitation.

While God allows for human choice and human choice can be destructive, he also gave us free will to decide who we will be. Princess

Warriors, God wants you filled with the rights that make you human and free. In addition to inviting you to be in a close relationship with him, it is for freedom that he set you free (see Galatians 5:1).

I often picture God as a patient Father who has all his unique and differing children—inquisitive, plaintive, needy, open, verbal, bold, outspoken—around a banquet table. He looks around the table with a heart of joy and delight. He adores all of us as we live according to our true design—happy, full, but, most importantly, free.

I have learned to receive his joy and rest as I become more true to his design for me. I love it when my children express their individuality and when they say things that are bold. God wants us to be individuals, to be set apart from the habitual idol worship of trying to please others. Like a good parent, he enjoys seeing our growth and development as our true self emerges.

When my clients laugh, cry, yell in exasperation, and come to their senses, I feel tingly all over—the way your body gets comforting chills in the sun after being in a cold office or home. These same people start to go back to school, find their career, set boundaries with toxic people, and are genuinely happy. They may be scarred, but they are whole and wise, and you can see the Spirit of God in them. Being blessed and being happy are the same thing. Just as most earthly parents want their kids to be happy, so God intends the same for us who are loved by him—far more than we can love our children.

### Personal Goals That Grow Out of Your Rights

You and I are warriors. Stasi and John Eldredge declare in their book *Captivating* that "God desires the woman's spirit to rise up in his strength. . . . One day we will be queens—we will rule with Jesus—

(Revelation 21)."[3] We exist as separate individuals made in God's image. Guided by the Personal Bill of Rights, we then establish goals that delineate the purpose behind the rights. Let's start with the goals of treatment, which we can talk about in this book as goals of personal growth, goals of boundary setting, or ways to return to the original selves God designed us to be.

We'll begin with basic boundary concepts. When work begins on a construction project, you see the area roped off with stakes and neon-colored ribbons. We are rebuilding a life, so let's think of it as the "how-to" of installing and putting into place a strong wall with gates, drawbridges, and a moat—all of which protect the castle grounds that we were born with. Each of these has its place in forming and honoring appropriate personal boundaries.

Christian psychologists Dr. Henry Cloud and Dr. John Townsend are known for their groundbreaking work in this area, especially through their book *Boundaries*. In short, appropriate boundaries are needed to establish a basic awareness of your self as separate from others. Cloud and Townsend have offered these three starting points:

1. The ability to be emotionally attached to others, yet without giving up a sense of self and one's freedom to be apart.
2. The ability to say appropriate nos to others without fear of loss of love.
3. The ability to take appropriate nos from others without withdrawing emotionally.[4]

Remember, we are taking the early steps necessary to move us forward in a process that will enable us to thrive in life, beyond the trauma. *The Post-Traumatic Stress Sourcebook,* by Dr. Glenn Schiraldi, provides a tool I use with counseling clients. A Princess Warrior who is thriving has certain qualities:

> A thriving Princess Warrior realizes that her life will require ongoing maintenance, repair, and even redesign. Her choices and behavior reflect that she is committed to moving forward, planning for the future, being self-determined, feeling joy day to day, achieving mastery, seeing the self as valuable, reaching out to others, finding meaning and purpose, being ennobled by the experience, nurturing herself. She is growing in the ability to resolve guilt; she is generally satisfied with life and is able to hold on to peace, happiness, renewal, commitment to life, and optimism despite the scars. She is able to receive and give empowerment, committed to physical health, committed to loving again, able to connect with others who are suffering and imperfect without a need to hide, able to enjoy her own sense of humor, open to possibilities, and more interested in daily life without the need for an "adrenaline fix."[5]

Sit with this description, and use it to assess your own life and development. What is going on in your personal growth, and what still needs work? Ask yourself, *What areas do I need to grow in so I can achieve the next level?* It will be helpful to write down the question and, if you're not ready to assess yourself immediately, leave the question and return to it later. Voice memos and notes also are good ways to remember ideas as they come to you. Roy Baumeister and his colleagues at Florida State University identified the idea that self-mastery and achievement promoted a person's health and wholeness. They found no evidence that high self-esteem made people better students, more successful at work, or healthier. "After all these years," Baumeister wrote, "my recommendation is this: Forget about self-esteem and concentrate more on self-control and self-discipline."[6]

This leads to one of my favorite and most empowering messages, borrowed from Mohandas Gandhi: "Be the change you want to see in the world." I can't control others, but I can master my own behavior through Spirit-led choices. I can be the change and treat others the way I want to be treated, for "God has not given [me] a spirit of fear [from which most evil is born], but of power and of love and of a sound mind" (2 Timothy 1:7, NKJV).

However, self-mastery and achievement cannot occur until we commit to doing a thorough infrastructural assessment. In doing so, we often find that systems need to be uprooted and replaced. Henry Cloud, PhD, in his book *Necessary Endings,* offers help in identifying why we struggle to prune what's dead, pull the weeds, and purge ineffective systems and "toxic stuff" inside us:

- We hang on too long when we should end something now.
- We do not know if an ending is actually necessary, or if "it" or "he" is fixable.
- We are afraid of the unknown.
- We fear confrontation.
- We are afraid of hurting someone.
- We are afraid of letting go and the sadness associated with an ending.
- We do not possess the skills to execute the ending.
- We do not even know the right words to use.

- We have had too many and too painful endings in our personal history, so we avoid another one.
- When they are forced upon us, we do not know how to process them, and we sink or flounder.
- We do not learn from them, so we repeat the same mistakes over and over.[7]

The pruning process is necessary. It forces us to gather ourselves for not only setting the boundary lines of our lives but also for identifying what must be cast out so we can heal. The difficulty that slows most of us down is that doing these things will offend people. They will believe that we have unforgiving hearts and that we are holding on to unnecessary misgivings. Other people are responsible for themselves, which includes their judgments, reactions, and assumptions. You can't control anyone but yourself.

## Hurt Versus Harm

For you to grow in exercising your personal rights, it's essential you understand some basic truths so you won't be held back. One truth that you must embrace is this: *hurting a person doesn't have to harm a person.*

I sometimes confront a client regarding her disordered thinking and behavior. Such a confrontation might create distress, but am I causing harm? Quite the opposite; I am showing my client that she has a chance to identify one cause of her problems. In the immediate context, it's uncomfortable and it may even feel like hurt. But the long-range goal and outcome are healthy and positive.

Short-term hurt is needed to help a person care for herself and create a plan that prevents further degradation. As you take charge of your life and personal growth, determine whether the company you keep encourages growth or stunts it. Are the people you spend time with supporting what is best for you long term, or are they harming your potential growth?

Christ never accommodates a person's unhealthy beliefs or habits. He has no fear about upsetting us.

Sometimes a complete stranger will try to disrupt your growth. I once was cursed with "blood guilt" by a man I didn't know well. He was standing in the foyer at church. I was reprimanded by the man's shaking finger and reddened face. He cursed me for having left my abusive husband.

Reading the book *Boundaries* helped clarify for me that I was *not* defined by another person's choices, opinions, or attitude. I began to discover that God saw me as separate from others, even my family. I was loved, enjoyed, and created for a purpose. I learned I was responsible *for* myself and *to* others. But I was not responsible for other people, how they felt, or how they responded to me, including the man in the church foyer.

I began to identify my emotions and experiences and to slowly believe that they were just as important as anyone else's. I filled journals with my observations and wrote out plans.

God speaks repeatedly in the Old and New Testaments about wisdom and self-protection that can engage compassion while never losing the center of one's heart, where God's will and wisdom live. It is counterintuitive that God, who made you in his image, would ever want you to be small and insignificant. Being small and insignificant does not reflect the image of God, and you are an image bearer. You are a daughter of God, a Princess Warrior, never small or insignificant or unlovely.

When my clients work on identifying the ways they have been in bondage to toxic people, I often use Patrick Carnes's list of compulsive relational patterns to help them see more clearly. The list (summarized below) helps anyone further articulate the way she became trapped in numbing disconnection from herself and enslaved in her overconnection with others.

1. Compulsive helplessness develops in childhood when the subject is in a state of learned helplessness. People in this state do not act for themselves until there is a crisis.

2. Compulsive focus on the abuser is the lost sense of self that emerges as a child cannot challenge the source of fear, leading the child *and ultimately the adult* to obsess over anyone with power.

3. Compulsive self-reliance has been touted as an American ideal, but the pattern emerges in homes where closeness and affection are avoided. Self-sufficiency becomes the subject's easiest defense against needing others.

4. Compulsive care-giving is a pattern that places priority on the needs of others in the extreme, leading the subject to be easily exploited.

5. Compulsive care-*seeking* indicates a person is trying to compensate for unanswered needs from childhood or as a way to avoid the pain of growing.

6. Compulsive rejection is a mode of avoidance, shown in volatility toward people who have disappointed the

subject. This volatility becomes a way for the person to victimize others.

7. Compulsive compliance is chronic appeasement. People say yes when they want to say no, even if saying "yes" is destructive, dangerous, and against their value system.

8. Compulsive identification with others is a pattern of living in instant sympathy with others. The subject may be easily seduced and suffer personal loss and constant chaos.

9. Compulsive reality distortion ignores the obvious and leads a person to rationalize, excuse, or minimize abuse.

10. Compulsive abuse *seeking* is in evidence when a victim of abuse sets up relationships to repeat the same patterns of abuse, while the intensity and risk may vary.[8]

These patterns develop as ways to survive conditions that harmed our Spirit-led identity.

## Living Out Your Personal Bill of Rights

If we want to discover ourselves and live our lives with authenticity, then we will disappoint, if not offend, people. There is no choice in the matter. If you continue to live according to the rules of other people, you will not overcome the forces that hold you back. Remember that Jesus refused to give in to the demands of others. He lived as God directed, and it got him killed. Be thankful for his example. If Jesus had sought approval on the basis of accommodating the agendas of other people, we would have no savior, no leader. He lost his life because he stood for God's truth and didn't back down.

Sadly, you can't avoid rejection and disapproval. Jesus, who fully understands the pressure you are under, invites you to cast your burden on him (see Psalm 55:22 and 1 Peter 5:7). And consider this: when Jesus instructed his disciples to preach the good news, he said, "If anyone will not welcome you or listen to your words, leave that home or town and shake the dust off your feet" (Matthew 10:14).

Trust God when you fear rejection and are tempted to think you are responsible for the happiness of others. Paul emphasized that "if God is for us, who can be against us?" (Romans 8:31). Because I belong to God, I have already won the victory over my oppressors, because the Spirit who lives in me is greater than the spirit who lives in the world (see 1 John 4:4).

## WHAT ARE YOUR NEEDS?

Earlier we introduced two areas you need to explore: *What are your rights?* and *What are your needs?* It is time to move from your rights to your needs.

Here is a list of needs to consider as you get started on your self-mastery program: physical safety and security, financial security, the attention of others, being listened to, guidance, respect, validation, expression and the sharing of your feelings, a sense of belonging, nurturing, physical touching and being touched, intimacy, sexual expression, loyalty and trust, a sense of accomplishment, a sense of progress toward goals, a feeling of competence and mastery in some area, contribution, fun and play, a sense of freedom and independence, creativity, and the awareness of God's interest in you and His abundant sacrificial and unconditional love.[9]

As you consider these legitimate personal needs, ask yourself,

*What are my priorities? How do I want to remember my time spent this week or this month? What do I need over the weekend that would satisfy my ache for rest? What do I need so I feel honored among my friends and colleagues, and how can I contribute to this honoring dynamic?* Create a list similar to the Personal Bill of Rights we discussed earlier in this chapter. This time, make a list of Personal and Legitimate Needs.

Like a home that needs updating, you might need to make subtle changes to your list of needs in some seasons of life. This could be something major, such as changing careers or looking harder at how your marriage is becoming more superficial. You might change the way you spend money or the way you respond to your health needs. Maybe you will name and set boundaries with those who are closest to you and with those who continue to mistreat you.

I want you to think and pray about this segment. Have a notepad ready for ideas that come to mind. Try not to edit out the significance of what you are experiencing. Write it all down, no matter how seemingly insignificant.

Many of my clients talk about how they minimize their needs. They often say something like, "It didn't seem worth it to fight for myself." They could be talking about standing up to their spouse, boss, children, or in-laws; expressing their needs; pursuing professional aspirations; achieving financial stability; offering their opinion; and so on. However, it doesn't take long for them to realize that it is worth it.

It takes courage, which is not superhuman bravery or valor. Courage simply helps you step over obstacles of doubt so you will keep moving forward no matter what. We can move ahead in courage because the Master of the universe lifts the fog and turns on the lights when we ask for help.

We do not wage war against darkness because we have our act together or feel brave. We stand as Princess Warriors, with swords and shields in position, because we have access to the Creator God who made us in his image. Feel the power of that. Allow yourself to think of what *your* courage could accomplish.

Over time, you will learn to hear God in ways you haven't in the past. The Spirit of God sends gentle alarms to my nervous system when I am in the presence of those who do not honor me or themselves. He always makes way for deliverance too. Sometimes that deliverance is immediate, but if it's not, he comforts me until I am delivered.[10]

I am not protected from the reality of the Enemy, but I am saved from contending against him alone and being left to suffer his damage interminably. Despite my scars and wounds, I am led with a promise and the armor of God to fight and stand for him, for you, and for my loved ones, but I could not do so before I stood up for myself. He will train you, as he has me, in the way you will go (see Proverbs 22:6). While he carries you in your pain, he will give you wisdom to fortify your defenses and hope.

I needed to experience a healing work of God in my life. As we overcome the effects of sexual abuse, much is up to us in changing thought patterns, realizing what is true about us and what is a lie, taking up new practices in life that grow our health, and living in truth. Added to that is the need for miracles of God's power at work in us.

*Chapter 6*

# PREPARING FOR BATTLE

The heights by great [women] reached and kept
Were not attained by sudden flight,
But they, while their companions slept,
Were toiling upward in the night.

—HENRY WADSWORTH LONGFELLOW,
"THE LADDER OF ST. AUGUSTINE" (1858)

Satan does not want you to define yourself by your true human purpose. So I urge you to care for yourself with everything you've got. God's angel armies are with you, but you must fight alongside them. You will be rebuilding your life at the same time you are waging spiritual battle (see Nehemiah 4:16). In chapter 5 we discussed much of what it takes to rebuild your life with necessary boundaries and other components. In this chapter, we will focus more on the spiritual battle that you are waging as you rebuild.

You cannot let life just happen to you. God designed you with free will, and that gift is one of the most effective weapons you possess. When you choose to marry your will to God's, you take the first step in defeating Satan's influence and power. God wants you free and radiant with his presence of glory and power.

And as John Eldredge has written, "This battle for the heart is going to take all the courage you can muster. Heaven forbid you leave that heart behind."[1] In this chapter we will find out what it takes to become battle ready.

The spiritual weapons that God supplies give us the starting point. Paul spelled it out for Christians living in ancient Ephesus:

> Take up the full armor of God, so that [we] will be able to
> resist in the evil day, and having done everything, to stand
> firm. Stand firm therefore, having girded your loins with truth,
> and having put on the breastplate of righteousness, and having
> shod your feet with the preparation of the gospel of peace; in
> addition to all, taking up the shield of faith with which you
> will be able to extinguish all the flaming arrows of the evil one.
> And take the helmet of salvation, and the sword of the Spirit,
> which is the word of God. (Ephesians 6:13–17, NASB)

You will need to engage your logic as well as all of your senses as you take a stand for yourself against Satan and as you get honest about how you will develop your life to live as God is leading you.

Your options for healing are as vast as the pain and confusion caused by the past. You desire change—and so do I—but our fear of change works against us. We all wrestle with vulnerability, and the prospect of change, even positive change, promises to take us into the unknown. Part of being vulnerable is not caring about the opinions of other people. You can't give in to the myth that those who seek help are weak. You have to reject the ways others try to define you. You can only believe your identity as God defines you.

I wish I could say that in my counseling practice I help people never feel hurt or distressed again. That, of course, is not the case. Avoiding hurt and distress is not the goal in rebuilding. You should expect to feel uncomfortable, confused, disconnected, or out of your depth as you enter this battle against Satan. Sadness and even despair are not a result of a lack of faith. Christ himself experienced disappointment, and he felt anguish to the point of sweating blood as he awaited the scourge and torture and his imminent death (see Luke 22:44).

Brené Brown, PhD, LMSW, has profoundly changed people's understanding of vulnerability. She considers vulnerability to be our most accurate measure of courage and the "birthplace of innovation, creativity and change."[2] Brown explains what I have been trying to tell people (perhaps less effectively), that we need to own what we feel and let it tell us what we need. This includes examining your motives for compulsive behaviors and asking, *Is this helping me? What am I trying to solve or accomplish?*

Remember that you have an adversary who hates that you have God's call on your life. Satan hates that *you are a world changer.* And thus, he opposes you and all you stand for. A favorite weapon used by Satan is to wound you in a pattern, as deeply and as early in your life as he can. Abused people commonly assume it was all their fault. They somehow invited the abuse, or deserved it, or were too weak or foolish to prevent it from happening. If you accept blame for past abuse, you are likely to shut down emotionally. If you take that route you will refuse the vulnerability necessary to fight Satan. Instead, you will distract yourself with efficiency, busyness, addictions, distractions, bitterness, paranoia, and perfectionism.

Hold on to the truth. You are precious and powerful. If you really got this, you would change the world and bring *heaven* into the torment of others. You would change the world around you. Your adversary will do everything possible to keep you from doing this. He will injure you in an attempt to make you ineffectual.

Jesus told his followers, "Be as shrewd as snakes and as innocent as doves" (Matthew 10:16). In other words, learn the devil's modus operandi, but don't be changed by it. Be cunning, but stay joyful, warm, hospitable, generous, and teachable. Is this an overnight process? No. Is it possible? With the Creator of the universe, anything is possible.

However, it's good to admit that it is overwhelming. You put down roots in the soil of truth one step at a time. As I was writing this book, I became fascinated with Navy SEAL stories of training and battle. A Navy SEAL officer told a group of recruits who were heading into the infamous training program, known as BUD/S (basic underwater demolition/SEAL), that most of them would not withstand the training.

However, the officer let the recruits in on a piece of wisdom that likely made the difference between finishing and dropping out. He warned them not to think beyond the effort they had to make at any given moment. Don't think even five minutes ahead. Stay in the now, and don't overthink it.

Just like in SEAL training, you have to rebuild your life incrementally, stepping forward . . . and then stepping forward again. But don't try to look too far into the future, as it can easily overwhelm you. You are likely to feel afraid and very alone—maybe even crazy. Be glad for that, because it means you're heading in the right direction.

Look at the task one step—and one challenge—at a time. Do not look beyond it.

At the same time, don't keep thinking about rebuilding without acting on it. Get started, leave where you are, and start moving. In the same way we are expected to begin physical therapy immediately after surgery, we can't just sit and wait to heal. A couple of years ago, I underwent ACL reconstruction, and less than twenty-four hours later, a physical therapist came into my room and told me, "Get moving."

"What?" I said. "I have six incisions. I can't move."

"Start moving your kneecap around, and bend and straighten your leg," she insisted.

"That hurts!"

Without blinking she said, "Yes, it hurts, but it's not harming you. If you don't do this the injury will control the rest of your body. Get moving and you'll get stronger."

In the same way, I want to help you get started, to get moving, knowing in advance that it will hurt. But don't let your injury control the rest of your life. You will cry. It will hurt, and you might think this will only make it worse. I promise you it won't. Let's get moving.

You are backed by legions of men and women who have gone before you. You are supported by all the healed female leaders who have looked into the face of a horrible enemy and come through the other side. They now are better mothers, wives, friends, sisters, ministers, and professionals.

Your legacy is filled with promise and hope. This is where we dig in, refusing to turn back and refusing to continue doing nothing. This is your time and your place, Princess Warrior, to do the hard work of rebuilding. You will take charge, and over time, you will reclaim what is rightly yours: your identity, your future, your health, your personality, and your life.

## PROTOCOL FOR THE SOUL

Going deeper and pulling out the roots of lies and self-protection (the birthplace of personality disorders, by the way) will launch your healing. To begin, look at the assumptions you have made most of your life.

With each assumption you identify, ask:

1. Is this leading me to heal up or seal up?
2. If I am sealing up under a hardening protective cover, am I living the life of a victor or a victim?
3. If I am living the life of a victim, does my perpetrator deserve to continue to exercise that power over me?
4. Do I really believe that I can take the power back and reclaim my body and soul, my life and identity, and move into the future stronger and more resilient?

Assumptions are powerful enough to determine much of what you think, how you react, what you fear, and how you live. Are you weak or powerful? Are you reactive or self-directed? Are you timid or bold? Can you decide now that you will no longer allow the perpetrator to determine anything about you? Replace destructive assumptions with the truth. Plug into the power that God makes available to you; be self-directed, not reactive. Be bold and decisive as you take responsibility for your life.

Are you going to let a violator tell you how to live? There is only one answer: NO!

As you take the battle to Satan, refusing to allow him the high ground, find encouragement in early victories. Take notice when you make progress and celebrate it. Build success upon success. But be ready for the battle to heat up. As you make progress, Satan will fight even harder to push you backward. If you fear that you are regressing, losing ground in this hard-fought war, don't believe it. It is Satan accusing you: "This woman can't get better; she's no match for me." He will do his best to extinguish your energy, discourage your confidence, and blindside you with more betrayal.

He is the father of lies, so adopt a policy of never again believing a word he says. You have the weapons of God at your disposal. You are a Princess Warrior, and God has already said you'll win the war.

## SHARPENING YOUR DISCERNMENT

Remember that Satan enters our wounds and does everything possible to make them worse. So, before you enter battle, I want to give you a plan to sharpen your discernment. You can't reject Satan's lies unless you recognize them for what they are. "Put on the whole armor of God, that you may be able to stand against the wiles of the devil" (Ephesians 6:11, NKJV).

The Enemy can tear us down from the inside if we have not kicked him out. Satan does all he can to make you sick with spiritual confusion, emotional pain, and physical illness (such as gastrointestinal illnesses, migraines, and overall aches and pains). We are tempted to buckle under the oppression.

But remember, we have a right to name this oppression and kick Satan out. We get to heal as we take back all the ground we have given him through lie-based thinking and the compromises we made in the hope of shielding our pain. Timothy Keller, the pastor of New York City's Redeemer Church, has said:

> Modern people are uncomfortable with the existence of evil, let alone the existence of the Devil. Yet, the Bible teaches that we cannot fully understand the world we live in unless we realize that there are supernatural agents of evil. But it is not enough to believe in the Devil; a Christian must study his methods. Satan practices evil subtly. He tempts and accuses people rather than overthrowing their will. Temptation is when the Devil asks us to ignore the holiness of God. Accusation is when he blinds us to the love and grace of God.[3]

Discernment is essential, but you don't develop it simply by acknowledging how important it is. Prayer and meditation are two keys here. And since these practices might have led to frustration in the past, it's good to follow a method to help you stay focused and present.

A part of my daily devotions is a prayer given to me when I was worshiping in an Eastern Orthodox church. It provides words to use as you process your life in God's presence. Finding a structure for prayer, one that keeps you mindful of God throughout the day, establishes a solid spiritual foundation for the battle you are about to enter. Just as soldiers would never enter a war zone without first having gone through rigorous training, a Princess Warrior needs to prepare her soul on a daily basis through prayer.

I have found that the following approach to God in prayer has fed my soul in ways I could not do without. In keeping with the integrity of the Orthodox tradition, there are italicized portions that suggest a certain number of repetitions of a statement or word, or to make the sign of the cross. The repetitions and other italicized directives are given not to force conformity but as a way to add a meditative pause to the prayer. The choice to make the sign of the cross is optional if you are not Orthodox or Roman Catholic.

### The Daily Orthodox Trisagion Prayer

*Having gathered your thoughts, make the sign of the*
  *cross, saying,*
In the name of the Father, the Son, and the Holy
  Spirit. Amen.
*Afterward, stand or sit in silence for a few moments*
  *until all of your senses are calmed.*
Glory to You, O Lord, glory to You.
O Heavenly King, O Comforter, the Spirit of Truth,
  who is in all places and fills all things, the
  Treasure of good things and Giver of Life,
  come and abide in us. Cleanse us from every
  stain and save our souls, O Good One.

O Most Holy Trinity, have mercy on us.
O Lord, cleanse us from our sins.
O Master, pardon our iniquities.
O Holy One, visit and heal our infirmities for your name's sake.

Our Father, Who art in heaven, hallowed be Thy Name. Thy kingdom come, Thy will be done on earth as it is in heaven. Give us this day our daily bread, and forgive us our trespasses as we forgive those who trespass against us. And lead us not into temptation, but deliver us from evil. For thine is the kingdom and the power and the glory of the Father and of the Son and of the Holy Spirit, now and ever and unto ages of ages. Amen.

## Morning Prayer

Arising from sleep, I thank You, O Holy Trinity, that for the sake of Your great kindness and long suffering, You have not had indignation against me. . . . Neither have You destroyed me in my transgressions. But You have shown Your customary love toward man, and have raised me up . . . that I might sing my morning hymn and glorify Your sovereignty. Enlighten the eyes of my understanding, open my ears to receive Your words, and teach me Your commandments. Help me to do Your will, to sing to You, to confess You from my heart, to extol Your all-holy Name of the Father, Son and Holy Spirit, now and ever and unto ages of ages. Amen.

*(and/or)*

O Lord, grant me to greet the coming day in peace.
Help me in all things to rely upon Your Holy Will.
In every hour of the day, reveal Your will to me.

Bless my dealings with all who surround me.

Teach me to treat all that comes to me throughout the
     day with peace of soul and with firm convic-
     tion that Your will governs all.

In all my deeds and words, guide my thoughts and
     feelings.

In unforeseen events, let me not forget that all are sent
     by You.

Teach me to act firmly and wisely, without embitter-
     ing or embarrassing others.

Give me strength to bear the fatigue of the coming
     day with all that it shall bring.

Direct my will, teach me to pray. Pray You, Yourself,
     in me. Amen.

## Evening Prayer

O Eternal God, King of all creation, Who has kept me safe to
attain to this hour, forgive me the sins which I have committed
to this day in thought, word and deed. And cleanse, O Lord,
my humble soul from every stain of flesh and spirit. Grant me,
O Lord, to pass this night in peace, to rise from my bed, and to
please Your Holy Name all the days of my life, and to vanquish
the enemies, both corporeal and incorporeal, that contend
against me. Deliver me, O Lord, from the vain thoughts that
stain me, from evil desires. For Thine is the Kingdom and the
power and the glory of the Father and of the Son and of the
Holy Spirit, now and ever and unto ages of ages. Amen.[4]

Prayer is part of your training, just like regular exercise trains your muscles and contributes to the health of your lungs and heart. Your soul is preparing to enter battle against spiritual powers, and before you take that step, you need to have established a discipline of meeting God regularly, and frequently, in prayer.

Now we will turn to the next steps involved in your preparation, including specific types of prayer and the need for discernment.

*Chapter 7*

# PRAYER TRAINING TO MAKE
# YOU BATTLE-READY

Courage is not simply one of the virtues, but
the form of every virtue at the testing point.

—C. S. Lewis

Hold up your head! You were made for victory.

—Anne Gilchrist

You cannot defeat Satan on your own. You have likely tried a number of strategies that relied on your own strength, determination, and perseverance. It's time to recognize that if you act on your own, you will fail in this battle. Unless God is fighting the battle with you, you are no match for the wiles of Satan.

In this chapter, we will look at prayer as a vital and effective weapon against the Enemy. Don't neglect or undervalue prayer. It will help you separate truth from lies. Without it you will not be equipped to enter this battle.

Prayer is a confrontation with the Evil One, an offensive weapon used in battle. Ask God's Spirit to guide you as you stand up against the oppression wrought by sexual violation. The starting point is the need for discernment. Satan comes disguised as an angel of light (see 2 Corinthians 11:14). We all know people who have been misled by lies and false promises, all the while feeling confident they were doing the right thing.

## THE POWER OF INTERCESSORY PRAYER

My counselor in Santa Barbara had been working with me for years, and my distress and loneliness were increasing as I was "waking up." I had expected that, with all my hard work, things would start to smooth out. I had been rereading the *Boundaries* book as I also read the Bible and journaled and cried. This went on for at least a year.

My counselor mentioned a Yale-educated man who was committed to intercessory and healing prayer. When I met with him for the first time, he told me, "I have been preparing for this session, and my spirit is very distressed for you. You are in danger. You will die if you don't make changes."

He got it. He prayed and noted that I was terribly abandoned and rejected. While he prayed, I felt pressure all over my body. Perceiving this, he let me know that my torment was seen by God. I went to him several more times, but what I was learning scared me. I didn't know how to simultaneously quit something, not hurt people, and take care of myself.

About four months passed, and I ended up in another prayer session with this man. He said, "Why are you still living with that man [meaning my first husband]? You need to get out immediately, or you will die." The prayer warrior looked at me like a father and said, "And you need to go shopping and be female. Be the woman God made you to be."

At the time I had been wearing men's clothing, and I had cut off my hair. It was the grunge period, but my choices were much more involved than simply following a style. I had never had reason to feel safe, so I didn't know how to cultivate it. In retrospect, there were some loving people, even boys, who wanted good things for me. But it was so foreign to my experience that I didn't know how to accept it. I lived amid rubble and ruin—my walls and boundaries almost invisible by the time I was wearing men's clothing and shutting down to any desire.

I didn't want to be physically attractive or cling to hope for renewal. I wanted to be dead to my senses. I didn't want to feel anything or have a connection to the feminine—the gateway that led to pain as far as I was concerned. Even something as simple as caring for my appearance was lost on me. But the prayer intercessor got it, spoke God's practical good to me, and said, "Go shopping." How remarkable and sensitive is God to all parts of our lives!

By the time I first met with the prayer warrior, my understanding of being "loved" meant being disliked or unwanted, because love was critical and violating.

I had lowered my expectations of God and everyone around me. The intercessory prayer and personal care I was shown began a slow and steady awakening that has changed my life.

## THE PRAYER FOR DECLARATION OF INDEPENDENCE

One of Satan's most frequent and most effective weapons against you is to tell you believable lies. The following prayers are provided to help you declare yourself and your children (and grandchildren) independent from the activity of his lies. I encourage you to know that there is not just one way to pray; however, these are my tried-and-true, go-to prayers for myself. Once, when one of my children was struggling with suicidal thinking, we used the list of lies for him so that we could see what he was struggling with. We then guided him through the prayers that follow. I hand out these prayers in my clinical work more than anything else—much to my surprise.

The book of Romans alludes to the fact that these guides are just a beginning, because "the Spirit also helps our weakness [distress and pain]; for we do not know how to pray as we should, but the Spirit Himself intercedes for us with groanings too deep for words" (Romans 8:26, NASB). As you pray, you are standing against Satan in the name of the Lord Jesus Christ.

As you continue in prayer and start growing in discernment, use writing or journaling to help give form to your new clarity. A good place to begin is by paying attention to the blank space. This refers to the space on a page to be filled in with the names of people (first and last), groups, organizations, or institutions that have brought any oppression or confusion into your thinking and feelings. These may be names of people you deeply love and consider friends. They may be people you trust and have forgiven. The point is not that you are stuck with the damaging effects they had on you, but that you are taking back any ground within that castle property spoken of earlier that *may have been desecrated*. This has nothing to do with harboring a grudge or being unwilling to let go of old issues.

Consider this a deep-cleaning component that, to the naked eye, may not seem necessary. Do it anyway, because injuries can lie dormant and then come back to life, causing further destruction. It's important to bring them into the light, name them, and make use of the power of prayer. If you neglect doing this in the hopes that past injury will simply fade away, expect the injuries to sneak into your reasoning when your guard is down. Satan will use anything he can to bring you harm. Disarm him now by listing names of individuals, groups, and injuries so you can deal with them in prayer.

## PRAYING FOR POWER

You are battling against "the powers of this dark world and . . . the spiritual forces of evil" (Ephesians 6:12). You know already the difficulty of this war, and you need to acknowledge that you are fighting more than just the experiences, emotional scars, and horrors of past abuse. It is all that, plus a face-to-face spiritual war against forces bent on your destruction. With that in view, use prayer as both a defensive and an offensive weapon. I adapted the last paragraph of this prayer from the third chapter of Ephesians. It's important that we pray using God's words and truth as revealed in Scripture. As just mentioned, the blank is provided for you to speak the first and last name of anyone who has purposefully or unwittingly brought oppression and discouragement into your life. Read this aloud as it is a statement made against the darkness, which is not spirit and cannot be communicated to by spirit-based or internal prayer–based communication methods.

> Father, in the name of the Lord Jesus Christ, I take authority
> over and bind this demon that is afflicting me, along with
> those under his authority. You, evil and afflicting spirit, I bring

the blood of the Lord Jesus Christ between you and me. Any negative words, thoughts, or feelings you give _____ that are against me, I bind those words, thoughts, and feelings and put them back on you. I break any evil curse you've put upon me or that you are trying to carry out in my life, and I break any evil soul tie between me and the person I have named. I take back all the ground I've given you, and I confess my sin, if I've listened to your lies, thoughts, or feelings.

Now, you evil spirit from the person I have named, I command you to go to the place the Lord Jesus Christ wants you to go. Be gone in the name of the Lord Jesus Christ!

Father, in the name of the Lord Jesus Christ, I ask for protection and ask that the Holy Spirit and angels who watch over me would minister so that I would receive your counsel and comfort and be healed of my infirmities to your glory and my freedom.

I pray that out of your glorious riches, O Lord Jesus Christ, you would strengthen me with power through your Spirit in my inner being and dwell in my heart through faith. And I pray that I, being rooted and established in love, would have power, together with all the saints, to grasp how wide and long and high and deep is your love and to know this love that surpasses knowledge—that I may be filled to the measure of all the fullness of God. Now to you, who is able to do immeasurably more than all I ask or imagine, according to your power that is at work within me, to you be the glory throughout all generations, forever. Amen. (The final paragraph is adapted from Ephesians 3:16–21.)

Since 1996, I have used this prayer during countless nights of warfare. Every time, it has brought victory and peace. After praying I have felt the coolness of God's comforting Holy Spirit. I have felt Jesus's presence each time I have prayed this prayer. I hope and pray that you feel the same deliverance.

In his brief ministry, Christ healed those who sought him and made it clear he was a God of mercy. Thus, this prayer has become a method for evangelism in the work I do. I give this prayer to my clients and have used it with an Iraqi immigrant who claimed no particular belief in Christ.

I would urge you to take a picture of this prayer with your smartphone so that you can access it when you need to pray at work, at school, or anywhere away from home. If your friends, spouse, family, or children are struggling, let this be a prayer you give them so that they can kick out the Enemy's activity.

## THE BREAKING OF CURSES PRAYER

This prayer provides an opportunity for you to gain control of the effects of sin, committed by you and those who came before you. A large part of it is about confession. Confession is not about condemnation. God never condemns a person who comes confessing wrongdoing and seeking forgiveness. Condemnation comes from Satan, the liar. Paul made it clear that there is no condemnation in Christ and, therefore, no separation (see Romans 8:1). Just as we can't separate one part of our body from our blood and our bones, we can't be abandoned by God.

We are children of God, adopted as heirs to the throne, and confession involves naming our sin so that we "shine like stars in the universe as [we] hold out the word of life" (Philippians 2:15–16, NIV 1984). In confession, we indicate our desire to come under the control of the Holy Spirit. It is the necessary first step in being freed from our burdens so we can be comforted and counseled by the Spirit's guidance rather than our own.

In confession, you acknowledge that you are free to leave behind the things that encumber you. I tell my clients that *confession gives you back control.* It operates off the premise, and truth, that you have the right to make choices based on your values, standards, and priorities. Confession is an act of your will, a decision you make to put yourself and God's truth in the control seat as you displace the lies that have influenced and harmed you in the past.

Decide now: Do you want to own this issue, or will it own you? The more you grow into spiritual maturity and the riches of grace, the more your warfare with the flesh will become clearly defined.

Remember that sin-based behavior can also be characterized as lie-based behavior. When we do not believe that God cares unconditionally, we resort to the lies we have learned, and those lies engage us in behaviors that lead us away from God.

The Breaking of Curses prayer is useful for disconnecting yourself from anything you have done or said to give Satan a stronghold in your life. It also gives you an opportunity to put an end to any curses inherited from the generations that came before you. The first ellipsis (". . .") included in the prayer gives you an opportunity to confess and repent of sins you have integrated into your choices and behavior.

For instance, a client of mine had a significant history of betrayal and humiliation, so in her confession she named self-reliance and un-belief. Another client rationalized her control over others because she had so little attention in getting through life as a child, so she confessed to self-deception and conceit. Yet another felt like she was lonely but took few chances to meet others and defended her choice to do so, so she confessed to pride and entitlement.

The second ellipsis in the prayer is where you confess the sins of previous generations. The Old Testament scriptures hint at the reality of sins being transferred from one generation to another: "For I the LORD thy God am a jealous God, visiting the iniquity of the fathers upon the children unto the third and fourth generation of them that hate me" (Exodus 20:5; compare Exodus 34:7 and Deuteronomy 5:9). We reap what we sow, and sinful, unhealthy patterns in our own lives influence the thinking and behavior of our children. Such patterns are often repeated by the next generation, which continues the destructive cycle.

Confessing generational sin can include the following: verbal and physical abuse; emotional and/or physical neglect; pride; wrath; sworn oaths; pornography; seduction; deception and greed involving money; disregard for children; divorce; abortion; legalism; hypocrisy; racism; sexism; arrogance; adultery; suicide; addiction to work, food, drugs, alcohol, productivity, or money; compulsive and deleterious people-pleasing; fear; lying and embellishment; destructive rage; and abandonment.

This prayer is a way to come before God asking that the effects of past sin—your own and those of your ancestors and close family members—will be broken. It asks that you be freed and that your free choice to do right in all instances is restored. Read this prayer out loud as a declarative statement against the work of the devil in your life and in the generations before you.

Father, because I have accepted what the Lord Jesus Christ did for me on the cross, I am truly your child. I have been purchased by the blood of the Lord Jesus Christ. Since I belong to the Lord Jesus Christ, Satan and his kingdom have no right to oppress me. They have no power over me unless I have accepted their lies, thoughts, or feelings. Father, you have known all my sins. If there are any unconfessed sins in my life, I ask the Holy Spirit to reveal them to me now . . . *(As you confess specific sins, it's good to start with unbelief, then the seven deadly sins [anger, lust, greed, gluttony, sloth, envy, and pride], selfish ambition, and vain conceit.)* I repent of them now. I ask you to forgive me. Your Word tells me in 1 John 1:9 that when I confess my sin, you will forgive me of my sin and will cleanse me of all unrighteousness. I not only confess my own sin of accepting the lies, thoughts, and feelings of Satan and his demons, but I confess the sins that were committed by my parents, grandparents, great-grandparents, and their families and ancestors to the third and fourth generation—sins that may have introduced curses into my life. I confess those sins to you . . . *(Pause now to confess, for example, the seven deadly sins; sworn vows and oaths; unbelief; fear; occult beliefs and/or witchcraft; divorce; greed; legalism; sexual, verbal, or physical abuse; mockery; abandonment; neglect; arrogance; prejudice; chemical or sexual/pornographic addiction; anger and fear; pessimism; and sloth),* and I reject any curses that may have gained cause to come upon me. I bind all demons that are commissioned to carry out any curses in my life and forbid them to carry out those curses.

In the name of the Lord Jesus Christ, I take back any
ground that would give a curse any hold in my life. Since the
Lord Jesus Christ became a curse for me, I separate myself
(and my children) from my own sins, the sins of our ancestors,
and from any other person, group, or institution. I choose to
appropriate all that the Lord Jesus Christ wants me to be, and
I'm asking you to make your truth a reality in my experience.
I annul any rash statements I may have thought or spoken. I
reaffirm my faith in the Lord Jesus Christ, and as I choose to
be obedient to your Word, accept your truth, and reject satanic
lies, I accept your blessing in the place of any curse. I reject
every evil word that was knowingly or unknowingly spoken
against me by any demonic personality or by any person.

All this I pray in the name, the power, and the authority
of the Lord Jesus Christ. Amen.

Again, these prayers are suggestions, to give you a place to start.
There is not one specific or best way to pray. God hears our needs even
if they are uttered in a single word. Prayers simply provide a foundation from which to launch your voice into the realm of spiritual warfare in connection to the reality and person of God. These prayers
provide a tangible method of gaining an authoritative posture "against
the spiritual forces of evil in the heavenly places" (Ephesians 6:12,
ESV), and they also help reconnect us to the loving presence and truth
of God.

## Chapter 8

# RECONSTRUCTING YOUR MIND AND EMOTIONS

Strength doesn't come from physical capacity.
It comes from an indomitable will.

—GHANDI

Spiritual battle involves more than just your soul. It also requires the engagement of your mind, emotions, and body. As we continue in the discipline of prayer, we now turn to the involvement of mind, emotions, and body.

We will use an exercise I devised by blending the outlines provided in Cognitive Behavioral Therapy (CBT) and Eye Movement Desensitization Reprocessing (EMDR).

We will begin with what you believe. As a woman thinks in her heart, so is she (see Proverbs 23:7). The verse could also read, "As a woman *believes* in her heart, so is she," since beliefs are thoughts that we think a lot.

No one who is healthy and sane holds a baby and says, "You have no worth, and you are the furthest thing from lovable." Quite the opposite; when we hold a baby we are overcome with affection, knowing without having to think about it that this baby is precious, glorious, beautiful, wonderful, and sure to do great things in life. These things are inherent in being human, created in God's image. But as we mature and as life throws things at us, we begin to struggle to accept our inherent worth and lovability. It becomes easier to agree with the lies that are told about us, and we evolve into these lie-based beliefs. Pain is a teacher, and very often we learn the wrong lessons from our experiences.

Over time, the lie feels like truth, and we accept it in place of what God says is true of us. Thus begins the emotional watershed and behaviors that reinforce the lie. We get trapped in a way of life that we hate, but we feel we can't escape.

Look at the following chart, which contrasts lies and truths. Our thoughts typically derive from our circumstances and experiences, whether in the recent or distant past. Use this chart to begin reorganizing your thoughts about yourself.

Use the chart to identify a lie that emerges from a triggering event. Then identify emotions that may accompany the lie. Surprisingly, even the most articulate people I work with struggle to identify how they feel. If I think that I am insignificant, for instance, especially when I find myself in a situation where that false belief is triggered, I might feel angry, upset, irritated, and annoyed. All of those are, at the right time, good emotions to have, because they help me know what I feel. However, in counseling we call them secondary emotions because my first, or primary, set of feelings might involve more tender and vulnerable emotions.

For instance, I might feel anger and irritation because I feel abandoned, betrayed, lonely, invisible, hopeless, and discredited. Most of us

## BELIEFS (Both Lie-Based and Truth-Based)

| Lies | Truths |
| --- | --- |
| I don't deserve love. | I am designed for love. |
| I am a bad person. | I am made worthy and lovable. |
| I am terrible. | I am fine as I am. |
| I am worthless (inadequate). | I am worthy; I am worthwhile. |
| I am shameful. | I am honorable. |
| I am not lovable. | I am lovable. |
| I am not good enough. | I am designed good enough. |
| I deserve only bad things. | I am designed for good things. |
| I cannot be trusted. | I can be trusted. |
| I cannot trust myself. | I can (learn to) trust myself. |
| I cannot trust my judgment. | I can trust my judgment. |
| I cannot succeed. | I can succeed. |
| I am not in control. | I am now in control. |
| I am powerless. | I now have choices. |
| I am weak. | I am strong. |
| I cannot protect myself. | I can (learn to) take care of myself. |
| I am stupid. | I have intelligence. |
| I am insignificant (unimportant). | I am significant (important). |
| I am a disappointment. | I am okay just the way I am. |
| I deserve to die. | I am designed to live fully. |
| I deserve to be miserable. | I am designed for blessings. |
| I cannot get what I want. | I can get what I want. |
| I am a failure (will fail). | I can succeed. |
| I have to be perfect (i.e., to please everyone). | I can be myself (and that includes making mistakes). |
| I am permanently damaged. | I am (can be) healthy. |
| I am ugly (my body is hateful). | I am fine (attractive/lovable). |
| I should have done something. | I did the best I could. |
| I did something wrong. | I learned (can learn) from it. |
| I am in danger. | It's over; I am safe now. |
| I cannot stand it. | I can handle it. |
| I cannot trust anyone. | I can choose whom to trust. |
| I cannot let it out. | I can choose to let it out. |
| I do not deserve. | I can reclaim my true identity. |

are aware of our secondary emotions like anger, but we may not be able to identify our more sensitive experience reflected in primary emotions. Naming the primary emotions requires that we feel more vulnerable, and many of us have learned to avoid vulnerability.

It is an act of courage to admit the primary emotions, but the point of this is to break out of silence and avoidance/denial. When you admit to the primary emotions, it is hard at first. Wanting to avoid them is a response to a lie of Satan. In contrast, God's truth is that you are designed to be intimately aware of yourself.

This list can serve as a prompt to help you identify and own your primary emotions:

### Difficult or Negative Emotional States
- Angry (secondary emotion): hostile, insulted, betrayed, sore, annoyed, hateful, offended, bitter, resentful, provoked (primary emotions)
- Depressed (secondary emotion): disappointed, disrespected, discouraged, ashamed, powerless, diminished, guilty, empty, disgusted, despairing, hopeless, regretful, trapped (primary emotions)
- Confused (secondary emotion): embarrassed, distrustful, skeptical, uncertain (primary emotions)
- Helpless (secondary emotion): incapable, alone, paralyzed, useless, inferior, dominated, forced, regretful (primary emotions)
- Indifferent (secondary emotion): preoccupied, lifeless, worn out (primary emotions)

- Afraid (secondary emotion): suspicious, alarmed, panicked, worried, timid, doubtful, threatened, cowardly, menaced, wary (primary emotions)
- Hurt (secondary emotion): crushed, tormented, meaningless, invisible, deprived, wronged (primary emotions)

After naming one of your emotions associated with a lie-based thought, it is important to note what level of disturbance you feel on a scale from zero to ten. (Zero is neutral and ten is severely distressed.)

After you assign a numeric value, notice where you feel the distress in your body. If the level of distress is seven, for instance, where does your body hold the distress? Most people report they feel it somewhere in their torso. When we experience heartbreak, we can feel it in our chests. But more commonly, I have noticed, we feel it in our stomachs, our throats, and our heads.

Among my counseling clients, I have observed that the heartbreak from rejection is held in the stomach. Shame tends to be held in the throat, which is consistent with the work of shame in killing our voice and trapping us in silence.

Remember that the heart is bigger than the organ of the physical heart. John Eldredge has written, "The Bible sees the heart as the source of all creativity, courage, and conviction. It is the source of our faith, our hope, and of course, our love. It is the 'wellspring of life' within us (Proverbs 4:23), the very essence of our existence, the center of our being, the fount of our life."[1]

It is important to name the primary emotions that usually are hidden between secondary emotions. And as you do that, identify where in your body the emotions are held. As you do this, you combat Satan's efforts to cause you to be unaware of your mind, heart, and body. He uses lies and negative emotions to create distress and tension in an attempt to injure your body. When you wake up and speak, you start to take control.

## NOW FOR THE TRUTH

After you identify lie-based thinking and the emotions that follow, turn to truth-based thinking. If doing this is difficult, spend time thinking about positive experiences in which you were given credit for your achievements, accomplished a goal, or did the right thing.

During my initial training I looked over a list of truths and identified with almost none of them. I never knew I could *know* that I was worthwhile, lovable, and successful. Despite my achievements, I still believed accolades and accomplishments were isolated incidents of luck and blessing—not due to my intelligence, hard work, perseverance, and commitment. The truth that I was worthwhile, lovable, and successful was not a belief I could hold in my body.

Let's use the belief that you are insignificant as a way to work through the list of truths. You acknowledge that you believe you are insignificant, and you then identify your secondary and primary emotions related to this belief. You assign a numeric value to the level of distress that feeling insignificant causes you, and then you locate where your body holds that distress.

In turning away from the lie and toward the truth, ask, *Is it* always *true that I am insignificant?* No, it's not always true. Then what is a truthful and opposite belief? Now is the time to check the list of truths.

The truth-based thoughts are God's thoughts about you and to you. Remember the earlier reference to holding a baby. It is not difficult to hold a baby and look at her tiny face, hands, feet, and body and know, inherently, that this little person is worthy and lovable, that she has choices and will be capable of great achievements, that the baby will use her talents and intelligence and passions for good in the world. The baby, without even being able to speak, is without a doubt significant.

To get back to the exercise, let's use the truth "I am significant" as a way to use the list of truths to negate the lies of Satan. First, think about times you felt significant. Maybe you had helped someone and she expressed appreciation. Internally you felt the joy and satisfaction of having been helpful. Or you might recall having received a compliment on your cooking, on your loyalty in friendship, or in something you created that showed your talent and personality. Think of three examples that without question acknowledged your significance.

Now, identify the feelings that arose in response to others having called attention to your significance. Go over these feelings again. If needed, refer to this list for ideas.

## Pleasant or Positive Emotional States
- Open (secondary emotion): confident, reliable, sympathetic, interested, receptive, accepting, kind (primary emotions)
- Happy (secondary emotion): fortunate, delighted, thankful, important, festive (primary emotions)
- Alive (secondary emotion): playful, courageous, liberated, optimistic, free, animated, spirited, wonderful (primary emotions)

- Good (secondary emotion): calm, peaceful, at ease, grounded, comfortable, pleased, encouraged, certain, relaxed, relieved, serene, bright, blessed, reassured (primary emotions)
- Loving (secondary emotion): considerate, affectionate, sensitive, tender, devoted, passionate, warm, sympathetic, loved, comforted, capable (primary emotions)
- Interested (secondary emotion): concerned, fascinated, intrigued, absorbed, inquisitive, curious (primary emotions)

Having recalled instances in which you were identified as being significant and having identified the feelings that went with such recognition, name the corresponding feelings and emotions. You might say you feel confident, grounded, peaceful, and strong. Name these emotions out loud, and gauge how these truths feel in your body. Assign a numeric value from zero to ten, with zero indicating you don't think it's true and ten indicating it's undoubtedly true. Then ask yourself where you feel that truth in your body.

Even if the positive feeling you have is the size of a dime in your body, pay attention to it. Notice the location or put it in a location in your body, and breathe into that spot. Give the truth permission to grow larger inside you, one deep breath at a time. Even say out loud, "I give myself permission to believe this truth."

## PROTOCOL FOR THE SOUL

It is important that you not see this intervention as a substitute for counseling. In addition to seeking counseling, it may be necessary to undergo a thorough mental-health evaluation for possible treatment with pharmaceuticals, vitamins, nutrition, and amino acids to aid your brain health as you recover. But as a place to start, these exercises can help break down the lies you have believed and show you a way to replace lies with the truth that God speaks about you.

If you do seek counseling, this protocol is still useful as a way to work while you are under the care of a therapist. I developed this protocol over years of work in the mental-health field. It combines different tools so that you are able to soothe yourself when a therapist is not available. It is an organized, step-by-step plan to get relief without having to develop your own system.

You and I are responding to the life-and-death mission of our souls. We are renewing our minds, our subsequent emotions, and even our bodies. I want you to have a protocol for how to work through the distress that you experience. If you are trembling in the night or are stuck in a life-threatening event, you need more than a belief that God wants to heal you. So here is a plan that has proven its effectiveness in getting the Enemy's lies out of a person's head and body. Included here are the Beliefs List, the Difficult and Pleasant Emotional States, and the Personal Bill of Rights (which we discussed in chapter 5). Each step is clearly outlined and tells you in parentheses which list to refer to.

## Activating Event

Identify a recent event or a recollected event in which you were hurt, left to feel unimportant, or shamed. It might involve being stuck in traffic, discouraging work dynamics, or being disrespected by family. (Examples could be you were passed over for a promotion, your friend discounted your feelings, you weren't invited to a friend's celebration, someone shamed you for not getting over yourself, and so on.)

**Beliefs** (Refer to the list of lie-based beliefs listed earlier in this chapter)
Still thinking about the incident you identified, what happened to your belief in yourself at that moment? Recall the belief you started to consider. (Refer to the list of lies earlier in this chapter.)

## Consequences

1. Level of distress: What is your level of emotional distress on a zero-to-ten pain scale? Name your number.
2. Where do you feel that in your body?
3. Name the emotions. (Refer to the list of difficult emotions earlier in this chapter.)
4. What would this normally cause you to do? (For example, do you act critically, defensively, passive-aggressively, and so on?)

## Disputation (Countering Satan's lie with God's truth)

1. Is it always true that you are _____ ? (Write in the lie-based cognition that you named above.) Answer yes or no.
2. What might an opposite belief be? (Refer to the truth-based beliefs listed earlier and the Personal Bill of Rights statements listed in chapter 5.)
3. Name one to three examples of good decisions, rewards, or areas in your life that support a truth-based belief about yourself.

## Effects of New Thinking

1. Name the emotions you feel in light of the truth-based thought and the related personal right (from the Personal Bill of Rights). For positive-emotions prompts, refer to the Pleasant or Positive Emotional States listed earlier in this chapter.

2. How true is this truth-based thought on a zero-to-ten rating scale (zero meaning that it is untrue and ten meaning that it is unquestionably true)? Name your number.

3. Where do you feel that credibility in your body? (If, say, the credibility number is seven, is that seven in your chest, your throat, your eyes, your stomach, etc.?) Name the location in your body.

4. If you are struggling to accept the truth statement about you, for instance, that you are undoubtedly significant, valuable, and so forth, what is your level of struggle or distress? (As noted above, zero is neutral or fine, and ten is emotionally and physically overwrought.) Name your number.

5. What will you do now? (Consider responses such as assertive dialogue, praying about it, and giving it time to marinate). Does this action support your values, standards, and priorities? Does it support God's statements about you?

Commit to a plan, whether it's writing the assertive statements you need to say to someone; choosing to get organized or to exercise; hiring a lawyer, trainer, or therapist; joining a support group; or taking some other action that supports these truths you are granting yourself permission to believe.

# Chapter 9

# RECONSTRUCTING YOUR BODY

Don't you know that you yourselves are God's
temple and that God's Spirit dwells in your
midst? If anyone destroys God's temple, God
will destroy that person; for God's temple is
sacred, and you together are that temple.

—1 CORINTHIANS 3:16–17

It doesn't take a laboratory experiment to establish the direct connection between your mind and body. Let's say your teenager is driving and you're riding in the passenger seat. Your teen feels confident behind the wheel, but you see that a neighbor is backing out of his driveway and not checking the street.

Your mind pictures a collision, and simultaneously your body tenses up. Your foot might start hitting the floor in search of an imaginary brake pedal. Your hand might grab hold of the armrest or dashboard. You are likely to yell, "Look out!!!"

Your mind pictured something that had not occurred, yet your body reacted immediately as if the picture in your mind was an accomplished fact. Without meaning to, you reacted as if the neighbor had backed into your car with you and your teenager inside.

Here is a more ordinary example. You're at a movie theater. The theater is full of fans who came to see a thriller. The acting, the story line, and the special effects are so real it's like you're in the scene. You hear gasps; someone spills her popcorn; you see couples huddle together during the tense scenes. It's a movie projected on a flat screen, two-dimensional storytelling with sound. But the audience is reacting as if they are being chased, shot at, or ambushed in a dark alley. The body reacts to stimulus—whether it's sight, sound, images, recalled events, or other external influences—as if the stimulus is real even if it is fictional, merely anticipated, or suggested by other triggers.

These are mild examples, but when it comes to the lies Satan tells you about who you are, the lies can have a damaging effect on your body. Because body and mind are so closely linked, this chapter provides you with breathing and meditation exercises to help clear the clutter in your thinking and produce tangible relaxation in your body. Dr. Herbert Benson's book *Relaxation Revolution* offers scientific evidence that mind-body practices can have powerful effects—in a surprisingly short period of time. Study after study, carried out with the most careful scientific protocols, produced incontrovertible evidence that the mind can indeed influence—and heal—the body.

Your body's response to stress is not a theory; it's easily observable and experienced regularly by all of us. Reducing physical stress is *mandatory* in promoting good health. In this chapter we will look at simple and practical strategies for your daily self-care.

Let's begin with your need for oxygen. That might seem to be an obvious thing to say, but too many of us cheat ourselves out of the benefits of filling our lungs with oxygen, the most important nutrient for the brain. The brain, while only 2 percent of your body weight, uses 20 percent of the oxygen you breathe.

## RELAXING YOUR BODY,
## CLEARING YOUR MIND

The pace of our living does harm to our minds and bodies. Our minds are cluttered with deadlines, duties, projects, and appointments. Our children might have to repeat a question to get our attention; we might realize at the end of the day that we overlooked an important thing in all the busyness. It's not just our minds that are affected. Stress gives us headaches, stiffness, stomach upsets, difficulty sleeping, irritability . . . the list goes on.

We neglect relaxation at our peril. Our minds and bodies are integrated, and steps toward health need to involve both. Learn the following steps toward greater relaxation, in sequence, so you can close your eyes while doing them, which will assist your efforts.

Find a comfortable and quiet space to sit, and start by taking a couple of deep breaths. Use the following technique to activate the calming process.

- Extend your arms straight in front of you. Cross your wrists one over the other. Put your palms together, and clench your palms into a single fist. Pull that fist in toward your chest by dipping it downward, then bringing it to your chest. This method is used as a treatment to help achieve brain balance.

- Rest your clenched hands or fist on your chest.
- Be aware of the middle of your body.
- Inhale through the nose with the tip of your tongue touching the roof of your mouth, just behind your front teeth.
- Exhale out of the mouth with pursed lips (or a relaxed pucker).
- As you inhale through the nose, breathe deeply to fill the bottoms of your lungs. Allow your diaphragm to move outward, as if you were filling a balloon in your stomach. Exhale and drop your shoulders, elbows, and wrists. Feel your chest widening and expanding.
- Let your exhale push the clutter of stress and burdens out of your body. Remember that cause and effect reasoning improves with relaxation, so you are not losing control as you relax. See in your mind's eye that you are washing out the grime of stress.
- Use breathing to relax all parts of your body. Breathe into your feet as you draw the oxygen into your lungs. Feel your body resting heavily into your seat as you exhale and purge toxic stress.
- As you exhale, let your shoulders, elbows, and wrists sink toward the floor.
- Use color to aid in relaxation. Breathe in through the top of your head a color that is clean and light. Inhale for a count of four, hold for one count, and exhale for a count of five.

- Alternate between breathing in through the bottom of
  your feet and through the top of your head. Remember the four-one-five breathing method. Do this four
  times.
- Take your time, and when you're ready, gently and slowly
  open your eyes.

As you take in more oxygen and involve as much of your body as
possible, engage your mind as well. Using visual images can further
develop the mind-body connection by engaging more of your senses in
the exercise. For instance, picture a scene of great beauty in nature, and
feel the love of God expressed in his work of creation.

You can involve your sense of hearing by playing a recording of
nature sounds at low volume. It could be songbirds, wind rustling
through leaves, or waves lapping at the shore. I have had clients listen
to the sound of a mountain stream.

## MIND-BODY PHASE TWO

When trauma is on the front burner of a client's mind, emotions, and
behavior, I use the technique that follows. It takes you further into
relaxation to deal with chronic and acute stress and to help clear your
mind and relax your body.

### The Forest Meditation

Imagine you are walking along a path deep in a forest, with a backpack
filled with sticks. All around you are tall trees: pines, firs, maples, elms,
redwoods, and oaks. The trees represent a protective and stabilizing

force, with their roots growing deep into the ground and their branches extending far and wide to comfort you.

You hear the sound of a mountain stream and the wind blowing through treetops. These sounds soothe you and allow you to be present in the moment. You can smell the rich dampness of the forest floor, the smell of earth and new seedlings and rotting leaves. Now you look up through the treetops and see a periwinkle sky. You notice how high the sun is. As the sun enters the canopy of the treetops, it breaks into rays that create intricate patterns of light and shadow. The forest begins to feel like a sacred space that fills you with a sense of protection, comfort, and reassurance.

As you walk through the forest, you hear the sound of rushing water. It gets louder as you approach, and before long you are at the edge of a mountain stream. You look at the stream and notice how clear and sparkling the water is. Imagine now a world of waterfalls all around you. Each waterfall creates a fortified shield that guards you against anything that would seek to harm you. Stress comes at you, but it's caught in the water where it is blurred, obscured, and washed downstream.

As you stand beside the stream, you notice that the sticks have fallen from your backpack. You feel less burdened already.

Each stick represents an element of pressure, distress, or confusion in your life—whether it is a person who has hurt you or a situation where a decision needs to be made. As you think of these things, you might feel ambivalent or burdened.

You pick up one of the sticks as you fill your lungs with air. You cast the stick into the stream and exhale. You release through pursed lips the toxic and burdensome stress that belongs to that problem. Pick up the next stick, and inhale through your nose. Throw the stick, and exhale out of your mouth.

As you release the sticks, allow them to float away with the current of the stream. See them float into the distance, around a bend, and out of sight. Take your time.

When you have completed throwing all the sticks into the stream, see yourself sitting or lying down on a grassy slope beside the stream. The sound of the stream reminds you that the sticks are floating away to a place where they will be sorted through. You have released those thoughts and concerns so that you may now relax and be restored.

This is your time to let go and, like a sponge, absorb the moment. You take in a deep breath of fresh air, finding the subtle smells of the forest very refreshing. Exhale and allow yourself to sink into the bed of soft grass. Continue to release any tension in your eyes, your jaw, and your shoulders.

The tension melts out of your body and seeps through the grass and into the soil. Allow the sights, sounds, and smells of this beautiful wooded area to fill you with a deep sense of comfort, reassurance, and protection.

### The Soothing Sunlight

Note again the world of waterfalls surrounding you. Stress may come at you, but it's caught in the water where it is blurred, obscured, and washed downstream. The waterfalls stand guard so you are safe to absorb the moment.

Now imagine that you can feel the warmth and light from the sun directly above you. The source of this sun is Jesus. The more you use of his light, the more there is. You can feel it shining down through your body. You feel the light of Jesus begin to relax and soothe every part of your body. His light will gently heat the tough and tight areas of tension. It will melt away all areas of tension stored throughout your body.

In a moment, allow the sunlight to move to your arms. Focus it there. Experience the warmth and light as it massages first your fingertips, then your hands, lower arms, upper arms, and finally your shoulders. Feel the sunlight loosening and widening the muscle fibers in both of your arms. You can feel it healing every muscle, tendon, and nerve in your arms as it melts the tight tension into liquid. The melted tension pours out of you and flows into the grass, then into the soil beneath it. And you feel your arms—from the tips of your fingers to your shoulders—resting heavily into the grass.

And, gently now, take the light and move it to your legs. Allow it to move from the tips of your toes all the way up your legs to the hip joints. Feel the warmth as sunlight moves up from your feet to your calves, then to your knees, then to your outer thighs, and finally to your hip bones. Feel the sunlight soothing every muscle in your legs and hips. Let the sunlight continue to melt away the tight blocks of tension in your feet, legs, and hips. The melted tension pours out of you and flows into the grass, then into the soil beneath it. And you feel your legs—from the tips of your toes to your hips—resting heavily into the grass.

Now move the light into your stomach area. Feel it warming and soothing every organ in the lower part of your torso. Feel the tension—of all the burdens, of all those who have not looked out for you or wanted the best for you—draining away from you. Your stomach and lower abdomen relax, and your bellybutton falls toward the base of your spine. Take a deep breath and exhale through pursed lips. The melted tension pours out of you. You feel your abdomen and hips and lower back rest more heavily into the grass.

Gently now, take the light from the sun and move it into your chest area. Let it soothe and comfort that area. Feel it streaming into your chest. See the muscles unwind and loosen in the space between each rib. With each deep breath and cleansing exhale, your chest becomes light, unburdened, and wide. The melted tension pours out of you. You feel that breathing is easy.

And gently now, you might bring the light from the sun down through the top of your head. Imagine it massaging its way from the top of your head to the area around your eyes and then your jaws. In a moment, feel the warmth of the sunlight moving down into your neck. The waterfalls still stand guard, and the trees are deeply rooted. They extend their branches above you so that are safe to release the defenses in your neck.

Now let the light move down your spine all the way to your tailbone. Imagine the light moving out from your spine into every nerve of your body. Feel the sunlight soothing and smoothing every frayed nerve ending. Let yourself enter into a deep state of release.

In your mind's eye, open your hands with your palms turned up toward the sun. Receive the work of this gentle and warming sun. See your hands holding the depth of the comfort of this moment. Do this while releasing any remaining tension. Again, allow the sun to send its melting warmth. See the remaining tension flow away from your body into the grass and soil beneath you.

Inhale deeply into your lungs, and continue to exhale any remaining tension into a bubble in front of you. As you exhale through pursed lips, see a cloud of toxic pain leave your body. When you have completed this, see the bubble float far from you. Now it may be so far from you that it's only a speck, and eventually it is gone entirely from sight.

See now that you are growing your wisdom to accept the truth of who you are without the distress that often distracts and burdens you. You are growing your wisdom to let go of what you cannot control. You are achieving separateness from the burdens and relearning freedom from fear. Your brain is absorbing this.

Accept a color that represents the reassurance and peace of this moment. Give this color permission to fill your entire body. Allow it to emanate from your body and become a translucent shield that protects and soothes you. Carry this color into your day. See yourself accepting this color and all that it brings you as you respond to the various events of the day.

Inhale a final time. Take in the object at the farthest distance in the room. Slowly bring your eyes to your hands. And now look directly in front of you.

To help you embrace these meditations more completely, record yourself reading the text, or ask a loved one to record the text. Use a calm voice and a moderate tempo. There is no rush necessary. Then listen to the recording and allow yourself to move more fully into the experience.

*Chapter 10*

# WHAT TO DO WHEN YOU DOUBT GOD

My ears had heard of you
  but now my eyes have seen you.
—Job, speaking to God (Job 42:5)

Do not go gentle into that good night, . . .
Rage, rage against the dying of the light.
—Dylan Thomas

In 1998 I had an experience with God that changed what I knew of him. I was twenty-seven years old and had graduated from Columbia University. I was divorced from my first husband, and I had changed my name and gathered myself for newfound freedom. For as long as I could remember, I had been submerged under other people's needs. It was time for me to be present to myself, my moments, and my expectations.

I didn't realize that finally I was finding new freedom as well as my voice. Neither did I realize that I would undergo a season that would redefine how God wanted to grow my trust. (I wasn't even aware that I lacked trust.) Doubt and fear needed to be released, and what better way to make that happen than to tell God off?

To this wounded soul, it was the only way I could heal. As you read a bit of my story, it's likely you will see similarities to your own experience. Like me, you could be struggling with issues and not identifying the underlying causes.

I was in Colorado, in the foothills of the Rocky Mountains, when I realized I could scream at God. I had hiked down an embankment near a stream. The weather was freezing, I was not dressed for it, and I marched into a clearing, expecting (almost wanting) to be struck by lightning.

The expectation of lightning had to do with what I was screaming. "God! How dare you! How dare you have expectations of me! How unthinkable that you always need me to be okay! How dare you for not giving back to me all I have given you! Where is the redemption? Where is the moment *I* feel some relief? When do *I* get to have my Cinderella story? When does something compensate for me? When am *I* not the superhero, always fine, always sunny and strong? *I* can't take it! *I* am done!"

There were no lightning bolts. In fact, even as I assumed I had lost all merit, this was the first time I really forced myself to believe that God was truly my Father. He showed me nothing but a gentle, warm, and enveloping presence. God, my Father, was soothing me. My good Father saw me in a psychological whirlwind, hurting deeply; and he said in a calming, soothing tone, *"Mary Ellen, Mary Ellen, I am here. It's okay. It's going to be okay."*

Have you heard words to that effect from your Father? Do you trust him enough to scream at him, unleashing your disappointment, frustration, hurt, and anger at his seeming inaction?

I had lived amid threats—both perceived and real—and fear had overtaken me. Realizing the destruction caused by fear, I let myself feel hot rage that melted my numbness. My ability to trust was slowly restored over the next decade.

Years of wrong assumptions and insidious lies were purged in my screaming rage. The best way to describe it is to compare it to the exhaustion mixed with relief that you feel after a fever breaks. I literally ached from the relief. I felt my back and core unwind from the tightening grip and heavy weight I had been carrying every day. Still, I was hurt, so very hurt.

I was about to begin learning life-changing truths about God's ways, his parenting and advocacy, his fight for me, his comfort, and his redemption. I was lovable. I was safe. I was his girl.

## MY BATTLE ON THE FRONT LINE

Growing up, I learned that love was an equation. You smile through pain and misfortune, and you are more wanted. You quote Scripture that supports God's purposes and lessons to be learned, and you get a relieved smile back that says, "There you go. You're going to be fine."

I couldn't separate the constant presence of pain from the Christian context of my life. The two existed as inseparable partners in my mind, which helps explain why it was so difficult for me to finally express my rage at God. But God came through for me, telling me: *"Your anger means you're alive. Not only will I draw toward you, but you will finally hear me instead of all the insulting window dressings of platitudes and pontifications. Your anger engages me, and I designed you to feel the strength that rises in your soul and body. Not only do I not judge you for your anger, your faithless skepticism, or your lack of vision and acceptance, but I am relieved that you finally trust me enough to feel those things in full awareness of me. With me, you get to stand for something. And, most of the time, the place to begin taking a stand is for yourself."*

Beginning at age eighteen, I engaged in an internal battle between who I understood myself to be and what was played out in my nightmares. For years I slept with a light on, listening to Scripture readings on CD with Christian worship music playing. I had to pray warfare prayers and often slept with my Bible on my chest. Lights on. Christian music playing. Bible touching me. It was a nightly battle.

There were times when my body would pop into a sitting position. I would feel as if I had been wrestling against some force. Something had been on me, stifling my breathing, silencing my voice. As I lay immobilized and terrified, only the name of Jesus Christ saved me. This is not some experiment I hoped would work. It was frontline battle, and the only weapon I really had was calling out "Jesus Christ."

I prided myself on being a studied and steady Christian who didn't resort to emotionality or contrived wisdom. I wasn't one to cry out in desperation. Even crying the name of Jesus Christ to suspend the agony of my nightmares was a new frontier. I did not foresee that I would actively pray against demonic activity, using warfare prayers to break oppression in current or past relationships and to lift the weight of family sin. I was being prepared, however, as a desperate believer in God.

## THE BAD GETS WORSE

During the spring of 1991, the torment was hotter and the confusion darker than I had known before. I quickly memorized Psalm 63.

I needed God more than ever, but I didn't even know how to picture him. I felt I had to open my prayers with apologies. "Sorry that . . . Because I should have . . . and I know you ask that I . . . so I hope you still like me and all. So please help me with . . . though I know you don't really like me." For years I filled journals with that basic score.

Despite my low self-esteem and cavernous uncertainty of God's love, I longed for God to be safe. I wished for an experiential friendship where God would be safe and calm, like a modern-day shepherd. Believing myself to be unwanted by God, I assumed there must be something wrong with me.

I imagine you might have fought off the darkness at night, desperately needing peace and rest and never feeling like you could escape danger. I suspect that you, like me, sought refuge in God only to feel that he had other people to attend to who were more deserving, or more pure, or more likable. What I am about to share might help you.

In spite of my dependence on the Bible, prayer, and the name of Jesus for protection from the forces that tried to smother me, things kept getting darker. My life was filled with betrayal and abandonment. My prayer time and relationship with God went from "He resents me, but I need him, so I have to keep trying" to a sordid, dark, sexual battle zone. When I closed my eyes or even visualized with my eyes open that God was listening to my prayers, I cringingly entered a state of anguish. I envisioned that God would choose not to listen to my prayers unless I performed sexual favors.

That is how broken I was, that I believed my value to anyone else—God included—was determined by something sexual. In an attempt to survive this new darkness, I developed a way to see God as a stream in the mountains. When that was ruined by invading thoughts, I tried to imagine him in symbols from nature, such as a dove of peace, a rainbow, or a majestic mountain scene. If the *personhood* of God in Jesus Christ emerged, I went back to the cringing, the battle, and the wish that it would all stop.

God as a Person was too much for me to deal with. It turned to chaos, and I had no emotional or spiritual tools to handle it.

I became more embittered and guarded. I believed God didn't care, only that he was trying to teach me something. The necessary lesson seemed clear to everyone but me. I knew that if I told people about this cringe-worthy, sad dynamic I had with God, I would be seen as foul, even deranged.

I know your experience is not identical to mine, but the stories I hear from clients show that certain patterns are consistent from one survivor to another. While the details differ, many of the struggles, confusion, questions, and pain are identical. In my life, pain was showing up in my spiritual disconnection.

Much is made in our culture over evil. It is said to be a fabrication, a holdover from the time of superstition and manufactured gods. It is said that evil is not the sinister spiritual force many believe it to be. Let me assure you, evil exists and it is somehow concentrated in Satan's attempts to destroy God's daughters through sexual violation. For years, Satan ruled my interpretation of God. It didn't matter how much I prayed or how much I said or did nice things for God. By every standard, I was living the American ideal—academically, socially, and physically. I won awards and received special-recognition trophies. I was a strong student and athlete and was recognized for being an achiever and leader.

But for all the appearance of sunny normalcy, I was being abused and harassed by men in leadership. As I mentioned earlier, it happened in my family, in my church, in my youth group, and at the two high schools I attended. I was ogled and flirted with, hugged and kissed too long, and lightly fondled (as though it were by accident). Almost every day I was either being sexualized or I was hearing the objectifying or raunchy things men had to say about women. All of these incidents happened at the hands of married Christian men in leadership positions in my high school and college, and from family members and the fathers of church friends.

Before I left for my freshman year of college, I was pursued by my youth pastor, who was ten years my elder. Even though he took all the initiative, I was judged for dating him. I was eighteen years old with a lifetime of broken boundaries in my head, so I took the blame and felt humiliated.

In college it all started again, in the midst of my family's collapse. I was sexually harassed by one professor and emotionally manipulated and disempowered (with undeserved low grades) by another professor, who was defending his abusive colleague.

All of this ran in tandem with abuse and neglect I suffered as a young married woman. The salt in this ever-widening wound was that, as word got out about the breakdown of my family of origin, we were abandoned in our long-established church relationships.

By the end of college and for a few years thereafter, I was so wounded that I now realize I had subconsciously *assumed* God must be like all these leering and abusive men and unsupportive friends. Most of my predators and betrayers were "Christian" men in trusted leadership positions.

Even while I waged a nightly battle for safety, the name of Jesus Christ—a highly controversial reality in my experience, and a doubted and disgusting disconnection according to occurrences in my life at that time—was the name that saved me.

During the night, my subconscious was awakened, and my self-protective, self-reliant, ever-busy self couldn't defend against it. Nighttime was the only time my body wasn't distracted from my subconscious awareness that my childhood and young-adult life were filled with landmines of threat, of violation, and of something that wanted me voiceless, if not dead. It was all so integrated into my life that it has taken years to grasp the wound that was left behind.

I would fall prey to the devil's schemes. I wasn't doing anything overtly ungodly, such as cheating on taxes or a spouse. I hadn't disclaimed God at all, and in fact, I worked the redemption of Christ into my story in my personal relationships and claimed it openly as the motive for my professional focus.

As I was growing up, my inner little girl wanted adoration, to be precious and lovable, but my whole self was embattled with the insecurity that it was never enough. As an adult who began to grow into the wholeness that was always there, I began to think as a free and healed woman. I began to trust my instincts.

## OUR DIVINE ALLY IN SPIRITUAL BATTLE

I now know that the Holy Spirit was fighting for me to disconnect from the many people who were betraying my trust. Although 1998 was a climactic meltdown of my mistaken beliefs, God had started to teach me nearly ten years prior to refuse to be played like a pawn. I had been working through the lies, much like one peels off onion layers or travels a maze that is formed of concentric circles. The first layer surrounding my anger was a battle for significance and worth, during my marriage to a man who I now realize never loved me. The second was my fight to protect future female students at the college I had graduated from. I was determined to do everything I could, after enduring nearly four years of sexual harassment and stalking, to have the man responsible removed. And finally, the last layer involved my deep fight against God for leading me on, or so I thought.

Today the anger speaks through a stomach that tightens at knowing that the Spirit of God is nudging me with a warning to pay attention. Since my early life taught me not to pay attention, I am getting back to my core identity by cutting through ever-thinner layers.

I have achieved comfort in the process of becoming truer to the original intent of my being—to love God from a whole heart that knows that I am a Princess Warrior made in his image, royal and eternally important.

As I live in truth, I refuse to absorb people's agendas, answer questions I don't believe would be wise to answer, laugh at a joke that I think is prurient or rude, or say yes when I want or need to say no.

As a result of living as the woman God made me to be, I have been threatened, rejected, and misunderstood. Since God made us separate through the boundary of skin and physicality, it also stands to reason that I am responsible not for the choices of others but only for my own. Anger clarifies this by stating, "I am mine."

A passage in the book *Boundaries,* by Drs. Henry Cloud and John Townsend, inspires my understanding of how anger helps to teach us our value and identity apart from others.

> Anger is a friend. It was created by God for a purpose: to tell us
> that there's a problem that needs to be confronted. Anger is a
> way for children to know that their experience is different from
> someone else's. The ability to use anger to distinguish between
> self and others is a boundary. Children who can appropriately
> express anger are children who will understand, later in life,
> when someone is trying to control or hurt them.[1]

Prior to my railing at God in 1998, I can't remember a time when anger or boldness was considered acceptable. But you and I know that it is useless to try to repress our anger at God over having been objectified, demeaned, and abused. I found that God would not allow himself to be associated with violation. Until I was entirely bold with him in my own defense, I would not ever really know him and would remain unarmed in battle.

Here is a truth I don't ever want you to let go of: You are made to be *intolerant of abuse*. You are designed to live according to God's plan for your life, even when it might impede what others insist is best for you.

## How Misdirected Platitudes
## Fed the Darkness

Christian adages had the effect of crippling my confidence. I'm sure many of these have worked against your own healing. "Forgive. They know not what they do." "Just remember all the things that person [meaning the perpetrator] did for you." "No one is all bad, so remember that we all need grace. You just never know what that person has been through."

Even when such sayings are quoted in an attempt to help, they have the effect of silencing the woman who has been abused. And not just that, but also of turning the tables to increase the guilt of a woman who is not able or willing to give the abuser a free pass. I kept confronting this line of reasoning, which helped keep me in the grip of darkness. Nightly battles continued while by day I was fighting to stay close to myself and hold to the boundaries I knew I needed.

It isn't expressed anger that changes us into people we don't want to be. It's unexpressed anger that does. Just as you were hurt in layers, you get to heal in layers. In 1998, in the foothills of the Rockies, God calmed me. And he did more. He said, *"Mary Ellen. Mary Ellen. Be still. Hand them over."* I saw an image of me wearing a trench coat. In the vision, my hands were closed into fists. Blood soaked the coat pockets from the inside out. I had been clutching beautiful crystals, and their spikes had cut into my hands as I demanded an explanation from God. While I wanted retribution and justice, the crystals were beautiful, bloody, injurious, and confusing.

What did the image mean? I was confused by it, but only for a moment before I realized what God was asking of me.

I had been taught that good works show obedience, which shows love. I was obedient: I led Bible studies; worked with marginalized teens; led fund-raising events for a crisis pregnancy organization; completed a graduate degree while struggling to find my soul; and handled a constant, high level of stress with aplomb. I kept my weight in check, my grades high, my friends carefully managed, and my family loyalty intact.

Keeping it all together was my bargaining chip. I felt that if I did my part, then God should do what I wanted. Essentially, I wanted payment for being faithful after all I had been through. The payment would come in the form of a man who truly loved me or in my reaching a place in life where I was respected and well-liked, wanted, and enjoyed.

As I gazed at the odd image of myself, I realized I had kept up the charade in which I looked faithful but ultimately failed to trust God. I had been holding God to the same demands that were always made of me: produce, impress, and reciprocate so that people will accept you.

## THE EVER-MOVING FINISH LINE

It's understandable that Princess Warriors learn to perform—by pushing themselves to be high achievers and obedient to religious rules, or by never letting the outside world see the turmoil inside. For many of us, holding things together was the only way to avoid the total collapse of our lives. For others, it was a way to try to prove to others and to ourselves that we were not deserving of the abuse we continued to suffer.

But now it's time to reprogram our minds and hearts, to hear the truth from God and to conform our lives to that truth. God did not feel it necessary to produce the results I demanded. I am thankful he didn't. If he had rewarded my demands by delivering on everything I asked, I never would have broken the perform-to-be-lovable cycle. God, by being God, stepped in to stop that madness.

Years later, I ran a marathon in San Diego. As I ran, I was picturing the finish line at a spot that was two miles short of the actual finish. This messed with my mental health. I was so tired at the 24.2-mile mark, and I had worn the wrong shoes and was in pain. I wanted to stop, but I knew I had another twenty minutes of running ahead of me.

This is a metaphor for the way I was imposing a lie on myself: *Produce to be loved. Impress to be remembered. Reciprocate to be respected and to belong.* God rescued me from this mental and spiritual trap or prison, where the finish line constantly moved farther away. I was never done striving for the finish line, never enjoyed the relief of completion, because I was doing this for people who didn't give two cents anyway. Quite the opposite: My striving served their interests. They could count on me to overdeliver, driven as I was by the wrong motivations. Why would they rescue me from that?

I cannot earn love. It's a gift to me from God simply because I breathe and have my own DNA. I am loved as a gift just for being here.

As U2's lead singer, Bono, sings, "You're the first and last of your kind."[2] Forgiveness is the exhalation to the inhalation that you take as you summon your senses to connect to the upset of all you have suffered.

Princess Warriors, we have seen the front line of battle. The instruction that you need to swing into forgiveness and trust that God is good fails to recognize work that needs to be done before forgiveness can be a possibility. For that reason, I will not ask you to forgive. And when you reach the point where you can forgive, you still will be wise not to trust. I tell my clients and friends openly that I love a lot of people and that I forgive them. However, the higher love is trust. And there are very few people I trust.

*Chapter 11*

# GET TO KNOW YOUR ENEMY

The thief comes only to steal and kill and
destroy. I came that [you] may have life and
have it abundantly.

—JESUS (JOHN 10:10, ESV)

My companion attacks his friends;
    he violates his covenant.
His talk is smooth as butter,
    yet war is in his heart;
his words are more soothing than oil,
    yet they are drawn swords.

—PSALM 55:20–21

Sex offenders can look into the faces of their victims and dominate
their will and individuality. The offenders are not harmed by the effects of their behavior because they carry a dark entitlement to rule
another person. Sex offenders believe that you, the victim, cannot fight
and that you don't know the difference between your person and their
need to dominate you.

How often do you hear a story about someone bringing horrible suffering into the lives of others? Or perhaps you think about the person who brought so much trauma into your life. The natural human response to such horror is to wonder, *How can anyone do such things?*

We ask that question because we possess normal human virtues such as compassion, kindness, concern, mercy, caring, and empathy. Because we would never intentionally increase the suffering of another person, we find it hard to understand how anyone could do these things. But remember, even Satan disguises himself as an angel of light (see 2 Corinthians 11:14). So it should come as no surprise that those who serve the purposes of evil have no conscience, no sense of human decency, no desire to serve the needs of anyone other than themselves. One way to begin to understand your enemy is to stop assuming that at heart he shares any redeeming human characteristics.

Now it's true that predators can be charming, winsome, endearing, and attractive. This is part of their strategy to get close to victims and win their trust. Discernment is needed on our part as we learn to identify and unmask what drives those who prey on others. Those who perpetrate are rightly labeled as sociopaths (people who lack a social or moral conscience).

Recent estimates say that one in every twenty-five people is a sociopath.[1] Not all sociopaths are sex offenders, but those who are will be what we discuss in this book. Most of these predators are never imprisoned. In fact, only 20 percent of male and female inmates are sociopaths, although sociopaths are probably responsible for approximately half of all serious crimes committed. The majority of sociopaths live freely and anonymously, holding down jobs, getting married, and having children. One sociopath writes, "We are legion and diverse."[2]

Sociopaths seek out different types of targets, from infants to children to adolescents to adults. The predator could be someone who assaults a girl on a date, his spouse, a coworker or neighbor, or a younger person he has authority over as a coach, teacher, professor, or another leader.

## PEDOPHILES

Jerry Sandusky, a former football coach at Pennsylvania State University, was convicted of forty-five counts of child sexual abuse. People who abuse children look and act like everyone else. In fact, they often go out of their way to appear trustworthy to gain access to children. They become friendly, earn trust, and gain time alone with children.

A sex offender grooms a child victim by identifying and targeting the child, who typically is vulnerable because of unassuming or preoccupied parents or caregivers. The offender gains trust and access to learn how to best approach and interact with the child. He plays a role in the child's life by convincing her that he is the only one who fully understands her needs and interests.[3] In this way, the perpetrator also exploits the child's empathy and convinces her that she is the only one who understands him.

He isolates the child by offering to help with rides or hobbies, for instance. There is secrecy around the relationship that is rewarded with special gifts and privileges, along with threats that telling would result in injury for those involved or those who know. Sexual contact is initiated slowly through casual touch that graduates to more sexualized touching. Finally, the perpetrator controls the relationship, communicating to the child that she is shamefully responsible for "making" the abuser do this to her. Sometimes there is a play-acting display of remorse and promises to change.

## SEX OFFENDERS WHO TARGET ADULTS

Much of the Christian world, especially the church world and many Christian ministries, remains oddly inattentive to the problem (and crime) of sexual violation. With many Christian leaders unwilling to acknowledge the severity of the problem, leaving those who are wronged largely abandoned, it is up to us to help one another—and to help ourselves.

Those who have not been victimized often wonder why the victims didn't remove themselves from the threatening relationships. They seem to think that predators wear a nametag that says "Hello, I'm Crusher, and I'm here to victimize you." But abusers don't announce themselves. They almost always are expert con men; they manipulate people and circumstances to get what they want. And they often move slowly, earning the victim's trust before becoming more controlling and then abusive.

It can be difficult for a woman involved in a romantic relationship to see the danger signs. A friend can often spot things sooner and can issue a warning. This needs to be happening more, and we need to take seriously the warnings of close friends and family members who love us and want the best for us.

Some women have suspicions about a man they are dating, finding him controlling, self-centered, hard to reach, untruthful, and so forth. It's easy to tell yourself that by loving him you can help him overcome such flaws. Don't fool yourself. There is very little you can do to correct the type of person who would violate you and then demand your allegiance. Why? They don't feel that they need help. Instead, they believe their way of being in the world is superior to others'.

A violator, once he is caught, will confess that his favorite part of violating you was getting you to feel sorry for him. If you take pity on a man who has major character flaws, he will use your pity to trespass all over you, your values, your priorities, and your other relationships. This fact is reported to researchers, therapists, and officers of the court. Don't pity him; leave! Even if he threatens to kill himself.

Here are ten signs to look for that will help you determine if a man is likely to be a predator.

1. He will make you *feel* unique, special, gifted, and enjoyed. People say abusers are charming, but they are known as "high warmth, low intention" people. You *feel like* they are on your side. However, once you make known your expectations—that he will be respectful, truthful, honest, kind in public, and so on—you will become the target of his mockery and even his wrath.

2. He feels he is entitled to claim you, your friends, your time, your phone, your social-media connections, your money, and more. He questions your friendships and your connection with family. Often he will arouse unwarranted suspicion about other relationships you have by saying something like "Your friend kept sneering at you while you were talking, like she didn't care about what you were saying. I'd watch my back with her if I were you." Or even

"Why wouldn't your mom and dad celebrate you more? I think you let a lot of people take advantage of your kind heart."

3. He fails to respect your personal space. He insists on hugging, touching, kissing, tickling, wrestling with, or holding you even after you have politely declined. And when you decline or restate what your limits are, he makes you feel embarrassed and stupid. He may also react by sulking or pouting, or he might do something to punish you. His goal is to make you feel sorry for him.

4. He is generous to a fault, but it comes at a price. You owe him now. He makes grand gestures to give the impression that you are important to him. But please realize you are not important to him; he is setting a trap. If this is happening at the outset of your relationship, be wary. Nothing is free, and trust and generosity should build over time in a healthy relationship.

5. When you don't do his bidding (i.e., by making him your top priority), he will sulk, stalk you, harass you with texts, or even threaten suicide. He will take to social media to bully you. He will say you're rejecting him "like everyone else in his life." Again, he is trying to make you feel sorry for him.

6. He lies about big things *and* insignificant things. Anything from what he picked up at the grocery store to his grade-point average in school to the sport he played to where he was after work. The best wisdom here says after

the person has lied to you three times, move on. The lies will increase and most certainly will include sexual infidelity.

7. He will try to convince you that the two of you share a sacred bond of secrecy and importance by saying that you and he are very much alike. This is an effort to dismantle any remaining barrier between you and him. If you give in to this, the exploitation will begin in full force. You will then risk your relationships, money, and career opportunities as well as lose confidence in your ability to trust your own judgment.

8. He manipulates situations so that only one person makes the rules, and the rules keep changing without warning. Here's a likely scenario: On Monday, you "should have known" that he needed you to call him. On Tuesday, when you call him, you "should have known" that he was busy and couldn't be bothered. On Wednesday when you don't call him, he questions why you can't understand how to love him. He will undermine your confidence by saying something like "It's no wonder people don't respect you."

9. Remember that perpetrators exploit your good heart. They know that almost everyone struggles to some degree with feelings of guilt, emptiness, and shame. Abusers read emotions like a newspaper, and they will use your emotions as weapons against you. He will crowd out your legitimate wants and needs to the point where there is room for only him. You will begin to not exist.

10. The neurochemicals associated with both fear and falling in love are similar, and they are especially addictive in a person who was raised to consider that love is dangerous. Love in unstable homes often can center on losing yourself and allowing someone to scare you to death. Admit to that, if that is your past experience, and don't try to reclaim the days of early romance. When you're dealing with a predator, the early romantic time was about setting a trap; it wasn't about loving you.

Now you can more accurately read the situation. Use these danger signs for early detection. Remember that true love sets us free. Love has nothing to do with control, subjugation, or fear of reprisal. Protect yourself from more-serious violations by reading the signs early and accurately, then take the decisive action needed to remove yourself from a suspect relationship. Remember, if he violates your trust while he's dating you, he most certainly will continue in that pattern once you're married.

While you are doing what is needed to protect yourself, bring in trustworthy friends. And if your own actions and the input and support of friends are not enough, I urge you to get help from a therapist trained in counseling those victimized by emotional abuse. An objective, trained third party can help you untangle your feelings, misgivings, and confusion so you can avoid further harm.

One self-admitted sociopath writes anonymously that she favors the following description of a sociopath from Hervey Cleckley's clinical profile in *The Mask of Sanity,* published in 1941. Cleckley distilled what he believed to be the sixteen key behavioral characteristics that define sociopathy.[4]

1. Superficial charm and good intelligence
2. Absence of delusions and other signs of irrational thinking
3. Absence of nervousness or psychoneurotic manifestations
4. Unreliability
5. Untruthfulness and insincerity
6. Lack of remorse and shame
7. Inadequately motivated antisocial behavior
8. Poor judgment and failure to learn by experience
9. Pathologic egocentricity and incapacity for love
10. General poverty in major affective reactions
11. Specific loss of insight
12. Unresponsiveness in general interpersonal relations
13. Fantastic and uninviting behavior with alcohol and sometimes without
14. Suicide threats (rarely carried out)
15. Impersonal, trivial, and poorly integrated sex life
16. Failure to follow any life plan

You know already that sexual violation is not limited in terms of one's level of intelligence, socioeconomic group, social background, education, or any other external descriptor. I grew up in an upper-class family with access to athletic clubs, country clubs, beautiful homes in Denver's polo grounds, and a condo in the mountains. I was a debutante, the daughter of two glowing people. My mom had been a county beauty queen, debutante, and president of her college sorority. My dad had been an Eagle Scout who was voted "best looking" in his high school graduating class. As we settled into life in Colorado in the 1980s, we became deeply connected to our church. The leaders of this church shared weekends in our condo in the mountains, as did the

Young Life leaders. We lived a life of sports, community involvement, achievement, beauty, and happiness.

What few understood was that our family lived in a harrowing unknown forced upon all of us by the sociopath who created two worlds inside each of our minds. There is the external world I just described, and the one that lurks in the dark night of his sociopathic soul.

The sociopath's premise is to dominate another person without getting caught, and it becomes their addictive chess game—soul against soul. They are not trying to connect, to share, to learn, to create. They are here to take. Here's the clincher though—they're charming, well-connected, accurate observers of humanity. They will tell you things you thought no one knew about you. You are their special one, the winner of their affections.

In my childhood, I felt that no one could love me better than the sociopath who was involved in my family system. While he was embarrassingly prurient in countless scenarios, he also knew the best occasion cards to buy. He gave the best compliments. He was the first to tell me that I had a mind like a steel trap.

My family moved up in society every time he made more money. We moved into more expansive homes and had more luxurious cars. He was the proclaimed "financial wizard" and continued his work in a very lucrative industry. Then my family lost nearly everything in the stock market crash of 1987. Consequently, we moved from a large home to a condo to a rented house to another large house—usually beyond our means.

One day when I was seven years old, I was playing with friends in the backyard. I had just moved to a new neighborhood. We were bouncing on a trampoline when the adult male from my childhood called me into the house.[5] I bounded in, suspecting nothing. He told me I had to get the towels out of the laundry room. I knew that didn't seem normal, but to question him was to be hurt. Soon I had my arms full of towels.

The laundry room was on the opposite end of the house, making it the perfect setting for domination. The towels were thrown out of my arms. The sociopath condemned me for not allowing my brother to play with me and my new friends. He went on to attack my intelligence. I was said to be "stupid" and "worthless." Then the beating began. I don't remember how many times he hit me with his open hand. My seven-year-old body was flung from one side of the room to the other.

After the beating was over, I was pushed out of the room. I walked past the laundry room, through the dining room, past the kitchen where other adults stood, past the eating area, and into the hallway where our bedrooms were. I must have passed out, because I awoke in my room with my pants wet. I asked my mom to help me change my clothes. But it wasn't until I began writing this book that I learned my mother asked the male relative what happened. He dominated her, pushed her, and told her that she was to stay out of it.

My jaw was stiff, and even now it hangs to the right. I have asymptomatic TMJ. My jaw clicks and tightens and cramps. And praise God it is not a major source of pain. Other victims of domestic violence are not so fortunate. I know them; they bear scars on both sides of their faces from corrective surgeries.

Hours later, after I was awakened, I stumbled to the dining room table, where I was made to eat dinner while sick and stiff from the stress of the event. My assailant made jokes as he played pool with my brother. He had dominated me that day. He was the victor, so he played pool and mocked me.

This would turn out to be an event that allowed evil to enter my innocent child soul. All the good, charming, and generous acts performed by this adult male in my childhood life would soon shift into a terror-based motivation until I was in my early thirties.

I started having restless anxiety as well as angry dreams of powerlessness. I was famous in my home and among friends for my nighttime outbursts, which often involved a sleepwalking-marching-around-and-yelling sort of activity.

Sometime later that year, I was pulled out of bed in the middle of the night. He grabbed my arm and slung me into the master bathroom, where he told me to drink the toilet water because I forgot to flush. I was so paralyzed by shock and fear that I bent down to do so. He pulled me up by my hair and, with a sinister grimace, said, "Don't do it again." The curse took root. I told myself that I deserved it, and I was rarely able to stand as a person on my own with my own voice. I became anything others wanted me to be, *because I was erased*. It was not until my midtwenties that I took the control back.

Martha Stout, author of *The Sociopath Next Door,* provides a window into the unconscionable mind of a perpetrator. They believe others are like themselves, "dishonestly play-acting something mythical called 'conscience.'" Yet sociopaths consider themselves "real" in a society of phonies. They prey upon those of high character, Stout continues, and have envy born of feeling hollow or empty. There is a thin inborn connection, which enables envy. It is one dimensional and sterile, all about destroying something in the character structure of a person with conscience.[6]

More than power, money, or prestige, a sociopath wants your pity, because "good people will let pathetic individuals get by with murder, so to speak, therefore any sociopath wishing to continue with his game, whatever it happens to be, should play repeatedly for none other than pity."[7]

## SATAN IS BEHIND THE SOCIOPATH

Do you see the attack of Satan? You, Princess Warrior, are the Trinity's special someone. You are gifted with a clean conscience and character. Satan waits to scourge you with his unmerciful attack on your soul. I am not on the fence about whether a spiritual battle rages for your entire self. The best method to end your hope, as far as Satan is concerned, is to hurt you as consistently as possible both physically and emotionally—and, dear warriors, as young as possible. What are we without our bodies? They carry our souls. When the heart of a person is crushed as the body is brutalized, Satan can manipulate and control almost all of one's reasoning.

One of my clients confronted her father, who had abused her with countless dirty jokes, exposure to pornography, and lewd remarks. Her father had always used his relationship with her to complain about his wife (my client's mother) and goaded her into his prurience by letting her know she was intelligent and strong—a compliment he did not give to anyone else. He was a Christian doctor and was well known for being gifted in his area of expertise. Although he had made lewd statements about many women to my client, it was when he made a sexual comment in reference to her own daughters that she pulled away. She wrote him about her boundaries and asked that he own his deviance and pursue help.

Her father continues to alternate between blaming and shaming her for the consequences of boundaries, and he sends texts telling her how much he loves her. He has never shown remorse, and he tries to make her feel that she is the unloving one for calling him out on his abuse.

A sociopath is not going to change. It is up to you to spot the patterns and put distance between yourself and the predator. Rather than spend more time looking at the evil done by the predator, let's look at the one perfect model for how a man should hold you in high regard. The opposite of a violator is, of course, Jesus.

## Chapter 12

# JESUS IS THE PERFECT MODEL FOR LOVE

> He reached down from on high and took
>     hold of me;
>   he drew me out of deep waters.
> He rescued me from my powerful enemy,
>     from my foes, who were too strong for me.
> They confronted me in the day of my disaster,
>     but the LORD was my support.
> He brought me out into a spacious place;
>     he rescued me because he delighted in me.
>
> —PSALM 18:16–19

You are given discernment as a mark of the Spirit of God so that you are cunning, without ever being a con (see Matthew 10:16). Jesus often had to perceive the thoughts of those who challenged him so that his response would speak to their motives and agendas, not merely to the words they said. Jesus sent out the twelve disciples to spread the gospel, instructing them in their authority and warning of persecution and trials. He told them, "I am sending you out like sheep among wolves. Therefore be as shrewd as snakes and as innocent as doves" (Matthew 10:16).

Jesus had firsthand experience of such opposition. He accepted an invitation to share a meal with a Pharisee. The Pharisee was surprised that Jesus did not observe the custom of washing before eating a meal (see Luke 11:38). When Jesus left the man's home, "the Pharisees and the teachers of the law began to oppose him fiercely and to besiege him with questions, waiting to catch him in something he might say" (Luke 11:53–54). Jesus had just been pointing out the hypocrisies of the Pharisees and the experts in the law. They responded with a siege of questions, hoping to trip him up.

You and I carry on a similar fight against those who have hidden motives and evil intent. But as Princess Warriors, we can live the victory that Jesus's resurrection makes possible. In Psalm 5, God is most certainly the ultimate Fighter on our behalf. No matter the extent of evil we are exposed to, we have his peace because he fights for us. We only need to give him permission to fight for us, then to act on our own behalf.

> You are not a God who takes pleasure in evil;
>     with you the wicked cannot dwell.
> The arrogant cannot stand in your presence;
>     you hate all who do wrong.
> You destroy those who tell lies;
>     bloodthirsty and deceitful men
>     the LORD abhors.

But I, by your great mercy,
    will come into your house. . . .


Not a word from their mouth can be trusted;
    their heart is filled with destruction.
Their throat is an open grave;
    with their tongue they speak deceit.
Declare them guilty, O God!
    Let their intrigues be their downfall. . . .


But let all who take refuge in you be glad;
    let them ever sing for joy.
Spread your protection over them,
        that those who love your name may rejoice in you.
For surely, O LORD, you bless the righteous;
    you surround them with your favor as with a
        shield. (Psalm 5:4–12, NIV 1984)


He is our shield and helper and our glorious sword. Our enemies will cower before us (see Deuteronomy 33:29).


## THE FULL MEANING OF REDEMPTION

Redemption—what other word better evokes hope? Redemption is never bad news. Look up *redemption* in a dictionary, and you'll find phrases such as "to buy back, recover by payment, to ransom, to rescue, to pay the penalty of, to atone for; to compensate for."[1]

Dear Princess Warrior, redemption's peace is an active process, not a finish line. It means staying alert to the movement of the Spirit's wisdom. Redemption is two things. First, it is a fixed state of identity that you are God's child, one of "a chosen race, a royal priesthood" (1 Peter 2:9, ESV) and a princess in his kingdom. You are officially his: "See, I have engraved you on the palms of my hands" (Isaiah 49:16). Second, redemption is a dynamic, ever-living state that shows up in the way we think, interpret, express, and act. The degree to which we embrace our redemption determines our habits and our relationships.

## To Be Brave Is to Defy

It requires bravery to defy the temptation to treat ourselves and others the way others have treated us. If I have been rejected, I will be tempted to reject myself, my needs, and my priorities. If I have done this to myself enough, I might wish I didn't reject others, but I will likely sour into someone who rejects the needs and priorities of others.

But when we turn to God, he says, "I will repay you for the years the locusts have eaten" (Joel 2:25). I assure you that he redeems the lost years.

For years I was told that I was crazy and worthless. God restored what was lost. He redeemed my life—all of it. Now my life is built on the total opposite of the years when significant people in my life kept negating me. I have to warn you, though, that as you heal, you will realign, change, and sometimes end past relationships. This came as a surprise and a disappointment to me. I had no idea that my healing would end so many relationships. However, there is cause for celebration, because all of my trauma bonds are gone, and God has more than restored my social structure with people who get me and trust that I have something of value to offer to others.

The redemptive work of God, even amid the losses that sometimes result, is brought home to your heart in his promises. I am here to convey that God's promises are true. "I will make rivers flow on barren heights, and springs within the valleys. I will turn the desert into pools of water, and the parched ground into springs" (Isaiah 41:18).

Think about Jesus's conversation with the woman at the well in the gospel of John, chapter 4. She was a Samaritan, a woman who had many husbands and now was living with a man. She would venture alone to retrieve water because she was a public outcast in her "impurity." Rabbis at that time would walk the long way around Samaria to avoid being defiled by the religious and racial half-breeds known as Samaritans. The story of Jesus asking the woman to draw some water for him is a layered story of forgiveness and redemption. It involves ethnic and religious shame and even the shame of a woman who had been alienated within Samaria.

And there is even more going on in this story. Jesus was also redeeming the story of Dinah, the daughter of Jacob and Leah. Centuries earlier, Dinah was raped by the Canaanite prince Shechem (see Genesis 34:1–2). As Jesus did a work of redemption in the life of the Samaritan woman, an outcast, he was offering redemption to all women who have been silenced and shamed after they had their innocence taken without permission.

The Son of God stepped into the middle of the shame—every layer of it—and announced total freedom from guilt. This was not only for the Samaritan woman. Notice that she shared her story of redemption with an entire village at a time when women did not speak in public. J. Lee Grady makes this point, connecting Dinah, the Samaritan woman, and women living today:

> Jesus answered Dinah's cry. . . . Jesus, our compassionate Savior, broke both cultural and religious rules to bring His miraculous healing to this forsaken place. He headed straight for the heart of the issue, stood on the ground where Dinah had suffered, and announced freedom. He found a woman who bore the same shame Dinah did. And there, sitting next to the well of Jacob, He poured His miraculous healing into her heart and set her spirit free. Today, He will do the same for any woman who has been abused.[2]

My wounded heart needed evidence that God was paying attention to my pain and to my struggles. I found that God's promises are trustworthy and they are healing. "Can a mother forget the baby at her breast and have no compassion on the child she has borne? Though she may forget, I will not forget you!" (Isaiah 49:15). We are built as physical people needing tangible proof. Write down the things you need to see happen, and ask for the special senses needed to detect them. Allow God to give you the vision to know what it is you need. As a separate exercise, note and write down whether you have experienced redemption in any other fashion in your life.

Only you can choose to trust God for your healing now and for your life after death. Jesus said he is the door, the only way to his Father and the life everlasting (see John 10:9). Jesus claims to be the only way we can get to God. The gospel message is clear, but it is inconvenient for those who prefer to think that many different roads lead to God. Some cringe at the apparent narrow-minded and arrogant position that Jesus seems to assume. However, it is not arrogance; it's what was prophesied in the Old Testament. This truth was included in the covenant promised to Abraham in Genesis 15. Humanity sinned, and God rescued us, but not by any other power, authority, or person than the Lord Jesus Christ.

"But when the kindness and love of God our Savior appeared, he saved us, not because of righteous things we had done, but because of his mercy. He saved us through the washing of rebirth and renewal by the Holy Spirit, whom he poured out on us generously through Jesus Christ our Savior, so that, having been justified by his grace, we might become heirs having the hope of eternal life" (Titus 3:4–7). Sincerity will not get anyone into heaven. Neither will good intentions and excellent behavior.

Jesus said in John 15:15 that he has revealed to us everything that has been revealed to him by the Father. Jesus broke the rules of society and religion whenever they contradicted the will of God. Jesus granted dignity to women in an ancient culture where women were second-class citizens. He connected with women in conversation and concern in situations that violated the cultural rules of the day. He gave high compliments to two people in Scripture—one to a Roman centurion (a gentile) and the other to a Canaanite woman (a gentile and a female) who begged Jesus to heal her daughter. Jesus was moved enough by their faith to say "I have not found anyone in Israel with such great faith" (Matthew 8:10) and "Woman, you have great faith!" (Matthew 15:28).

If you choose Jesus to be your Lord, Savior, and Hero, it will not wipe away all doubts and fears. But it will give you access to the greatest healing power ever.

Remember the man who said "I do believe; help me overcome my unbelief!" (Mark 9:24)? This man was responding to Jesus's statement: "Everything is possible for one who believes" (verse 23).

I am thrilled by this passage. Jesus honored the request of a man who loved his son and wanted him to be healed. Jesus healed the man's son even though the man openly admitted to a degree of unbelief. Prior to this, the man had brought his son to the disciples, but they were unable to heal him. Rather than lose hope, the man came to Jesus for his son's healing.

Jesus does the same with us. He ministers to us with grace, patience, and peace while we engage in the battle as we follow him. The lesson for us is that while our faith may be weak, what is essential is that we connect to the Trinity in total surrender.

I have worked with countless people who want the deep movement of God in their lives without releasing their wills to him. They want God to work, but they don't want to give up their agenda. But you must surrender your will and hand God the reins to your life. God will be there. We are designed to have faith—remember that. We put our faith in banks, in jobs, in exercise and eating right, and in higher education. Why not put your faith in the Lord of the universe?

Ask God for the patience to wait for him to show you what he wants you to do. Ask that he give you his eyes to see what he is doing and his strength to join him. Finally, ask for the encouragement you need to follow him in faith. He will be faithful and grant it to you, whether it's your child blossoming at a new skill or someone coming through with a thoughtful gesture. He wants to show he is there. Let him in—even if it's only a little. He will be patient with the little trust you can give, if that is where you need to start. The following verses show that God fights for us as we bravely open our hearts to him:

> If anyone does attack you, it will not be my doing; whoever attacks you will surrender to you. (Isaiah 54:15)

> Commit your way to the LORD; trust in him and he will do this: He will make your righteousness shine like the dawn, the justice of your cause like the noonday sun. (Psalm 37:5–6, NIV 1984)

> God is our refuge and strength, an ever-present help in trouble. (Psalm 46:1)

> Then they cried to the LORD in their trouble, and he saved them from their distress. He brought them out of darkness, the utter darkness, and broke away their chains. Let them give thanks to the LORD for his unfailing love and his wonderful deeds for mankind, for he breaks down gates of bronze and cuts through bars of iron. (Psalm 107:13–16)

> This is what the LORD says to his anointed, . . . I will go before you and will level the mountains; I will break down gates of bronze and cut through bars of iron. (Isaiah 45:1–2)

> And my God will meet all your needs according to the riches of his glory in Christ Jesus. (Philippians 4:19)

Let the beloved of the LORD rest secure in him, for he shields [her] all day long, and the one the LORD loves rests between his shoulders. (Deuteronomy 33:12)

Cast your cares on the LORD and he will sustain you; he will never let the righteous be shaken. (Psalm 55:22)

The LORD longs to be gracious to you; therefore he will rise up to show you compassion. For the LORD is a God of justice. Blessed are all who wait for him! . . . How gracious he will be when you cry for help! (Isaiah 30:18–19)

And the peace of God, which transcends all understanding, will guard your hearts and your minds in Christ Jesus." (Philippians 4:7)

You, Lord, took up my case; you redeemed my life. LORD, you have seen the wrong done to me. Uphold my cause! (Lamentations 3:58–59)

Know also that wisdom is like honey for you: If you find it, there is a future hope for you, and your hope will not be cut off. . . . For though the righteous fall seven times, they rise again. (Proverbs 24:14–16)

No weapon forged against you will prevail, and you will refute every tongue that accuses you. (Isaiah 54:17)

The LORD your God is with you, he is mighty to save. He will take great delight in you, he will quiet you with his love. . . . At that time [he] will deal with all who oppressed you. (Zephaniah 3:17, 19, NIV 1984)

I have told you these things, so that in me you may have peace. In this world you will have trouble. But take heart! I have overcome the world. (John 16:33)

## GOD UPHOLDS THE INJURED

In 1 Corinthians 1, the apostle Paul clarifies that God's greatness shines all the more boldly in those who are injured. Let's say I have an emotional wound that knows the pain of rejection. God not only restores the rejection with acceptance but also uses the pain to further elevate my awareness of another person's rejection. This makes me more believable and more compassionate. I can speak with authority as a survivor of rejection.

So it is:

God chose the foolish things of the world to shame the wise; God chose the weak things of the world to shame the strong. God chose the lowly things of this world and the despised things—and the things that are not—to nullify the things that are, so that no one may boast before him. It is because of him that you are in Christ Jesus, who has become for us wisdom from God—that is, our righteousness, holiness and redemption. (1 Corinthians 1:27–30)

While there is no thought that you are foolish, weak, or despised, God uses every bit of the things that have broken you down to build you up again—but better this time. There is greatness in the scar that will lead to your personal redemption, to the redemption of your family, your ministry, your education, your work, your parenting, your relationships. You can be better at loving and leaving a mark of generosity, creativity, ingenuity, and ambition so that you can be a strong place for others.

In 2 Corinthians 12:9, God told Paul, "My grace is sufficient for you, for my power is made perfect in weakness." The same is true for you and me. God's power is made perfect in our wounds. If I have a knee injury, that knee will likely become weakened. Yet with God's redemption it becomes an asset, a starting point for power, influence, and an organic and natural sense of how to care for others. What Satan intended for evil, God touches and makes new and better for generations to come. The following quote by Khalil Gibran is a reminder I keep by my kitchen sink and above my writing desk: "Out of suffering have emerged the strongest souls. The most massive characters are seared with scars."

Satan tried to destroy us using the people who abused us. Then God redeemed us. You and I are designed with greatness—valiant hearts, generous compassion, safe mercy, and fierce intelligence. Princess Warriors are, thus, world changers with scars. You bear the scars that display the Enemy's fierce fight against you for all the glory you bring to your days on earth. Golden legacy lies ahead. Let's look at ways you can attach yourself to the process of legacy formation—a golden gift to God's kingdom and those you know.

# Chapter 13

# YOUR LEGACY

It has been said that real freedom is about
setting others free.

—BRENÉ BROWN

Never forget, no matter how overwhelming
life's challenges and problems seem to be,
that one person can make a difference in
the world. In fact, it is always because of
one person that all the changes that matter
in the world come about. So be that person.

—R. BUCKMINSTER FULLER

Henry Cloud, a man whose work was used by Jesus to save my life, has
written: "Someone of virtue is a force, and a force always leaves a result."[1] Who but God would want you to be a force? It would do nothing but reward and glorify him if you were. Who but Satan would
want the opposite—that you are ineffective and without confidence?

Precious Princess Warrior, your legacy lies in the fact that you
picked up this book and said, "Enough!" You are ready to reject the

lies that have infested your head and your body. You have decided to expunge the filth of the wasted life that intersected with yours like a drunk driver slamming into your car.

## TRUE POWER

Brené Brown, PhD, LMSW, a forerunner in the exploration of the power of vulnerability, insists that we are meant to live in courage, compassion, and connection. We live in the courage to be imperfect, the compassion to be kind to ourselves and others, and the connection as a result of authenticity. Authenticity happens when we fully embrace vulnerability. Vulnerability is the birthplace of joy and love. Brown encourages us to let ourselves be seen, to love with our whole hearts, to practice gratitude and joy, and to know that we are enough— not too much or too little. Therefore, we say to others, "I love you" before they say it to us. We invest in relationships that may not work out. We engage the unknown without the precondition of a quid pro quo but with a peace in knowing that we are just doing our part.[2]

Vulnerability balanced with strong character breeds trust. For me to build trust with someone, I recognize that I need to be vulnerable enough for that person to identify with me. And I have to be strong enough for people to feel that they can depend on me. I can trust people to face reality with me if they are also balancing vulnerability with the pursuit of strong character, because I can be assured that I am going to be treated with respect and honesty.

Jesus attached and bonded to people by addressing their needs, initially calling himself the Son of Man. He made himself similar and

familiar first. It was much later in his ministry that he finally announced that he was the Son of God. He preached tolerance, grace,
and generosity, and he loathed legalism, which was filled with contempt and shame.

He connected with people in a way that made them feel understood and valued. He was accessible in his demeanor and his actions.
Can you imagine whether anyone would have given him any credence
if he hadn't done this? His claims were difficult enough to accept, but
had he dominated, demanded, remained aloof, or been antagonistic,
surely no one would have listened to him—not even to his saving
truth. Jesus showed investment, and then they believed. It's that simple. Too many leaders are legalistic and display low energy for people,
yet they expect to be respected and followed. I honor them from a
distance because they were made by God's hands, but I do not follow
them.

Princess Warriors, you are built to lead through connection and
investment. Make no mistake that Satan hurt you in these very areas
so that you would decide not to use these gifts. Reject the lies of Satan.
Because you are the first and last of your kind, no one in all of history
will be able to connect and invest like you.

## A FORCE FOR EMPATHY

If we are going to be a force for empathy, we have to be vulnerable
enough to receive it. Dr. Daniel Amen, a widely known psychiatrist,
wrote the book *Unleashing the Power of the Female Brain*. In it, he
discusses the unique capacity women have to be extraordinary leaders.

He notes that in general, women are designed neurobiologically to provide the following qualities of leadership:

- Women have more empathy than men do.
- Women have more appropriate worry than men do and are concerned with the welfare of others.
- Women have more self-control than men do.
- Women are collaborative and are able to bond or show connection with more agility than men are.
- Women have greater powers of intuition or gut feeling than men do and are usually correct in their assumptions.[3]

We are forces and leaders, which helps explain why Satan wants to destroy us. Your legacy starts with standing up for yourself—and this is work filled with dust, sweat, and blood. Standing up for yourself is a mighty and often messy act that is necessary if you are to depart from the people who brought darkness and confusion to your life.

I work with too many women who are afraid to let other people down, so they work around the pain of their abuse. They continue to interact with their abusers. They attend family functions where the perpetrator sits at the same Thanksgiving table. They continue to work in an environment where they are sexually harassed. They remain married to their rapist. (Husbands force sex on their wives far more than any of us would like to think.)

Until you take a stand that you will not tolerate the stealth attack on your soul, you will not be able to empathize with yourself or offer empathy to others. Consequently, your legacy-filled impact will lack effectiveness. Your power will be limited, and God's kingdom will not grow in the way only you could have grown it. If you lack self-respect and continue to entertain the status quo, you will not heal. Yet when you bring fear and shame-based behaviors to an end, your legacy will gain traction.

## BE THE CHANGE

Your legacy is like a one-hundred-dollar bill. It doesn't matter if it has been wrinkled and folded and even torn. It's always worth the same. Your value is inherent, endowed by God. Your legacy is what you choose to do with your value. After you insist on empathy from others, you give it.

This begins with how you treat yourself and your life. Do you have a drug problem, an eating problem, a spending problem? Are you using shame-based behaviors to soothe yourself? Do you still wrestle with contempt for yourself and others?

We can change our contempt and offer tenderness and understanding in its place. We can act as Jesus did; we step toward people when others step away. We show kindness, practical service, and emotional availability. We ask questions to check in and allow the other person to be vulnerable.

We remember someone's birthday by sending a text. We approach our neighborhoods, our office settings, our professional relationships, our children, our spouses, and our friends with encouragement and understanding. Kindness is never wasted. We can change the world by asking how one person's doctor's appointment went.

Mother Teresa once said, "Let no one ever come to you without leaving better and happier. Be the living expression of God's kindness: kindness in your face, kindness in your eyes, and kindness in your smile."[4] Contempt cannot exist alongside a kind, tender show of mercy.

For your legacy to reach others, you also need courage. This often means going against family allegiances, rituals, and expectations. When you do this, you will encounter anger, hostility, and rejection if you haven't already. There will be a price to pay as you refuse to please others.

To leave a legacy, we also need to identify and then reject our idols, even when they are acceptable in our culture. These include family, status, career, income, vanity, recreation, and chosen worldview. If we rely on anything other than God and his grace to *feel better,* we have a problem. If they "deliver" us into a temporary relief, we are worshiping God in form only.

Your legacy is sealed when you build up what was broken by promising to seek after God no matter the confusion, anger, or pain. When we stop carrying around our pain like it's who we are, we can begin to own that we need God to restore us. Then we can bring our gifts to God. Remember, God wants *you*—healed, broken, angry, lost, or found—more than he wants sacrifice. As Jesus said, "I desire mercy [for ourselves and others], not sacrifice" (Matthew 9:13).

Once we pay attention to practice being the change we want to see, we then float our attention to the reality of how this changes what we do with people, starting with our home life.

## THE PRINCESS WARRIOR AS A LEGACY-FILLED MOTHER

When Mother Teresa was asked how to promote world peace, her answer was, essentially, to go home, love our family, and remember that peace begins with a smile. Too many of us continue to struggle with the emotional expectations within our own parenting or the parenting we, as children, received from parents who were themselves violated.

Dr. Dan Allender, whose seminal work *The Wounded Heart* pointed the way for my healing over the course of many years, says two aspects are essential in a happy home. One is "being enjoyed for who one is rather than for what one does," and the second is being respected in your "uniqueness and separateness from other members of the family."[5] In families where abuse and violation take place, "the child is (to some degree) empty, alone, committed to pleasing, boundary-less, burdened."[6] Such a child is more susceptible to abuse because she craves intimacy, belonging, warmth, and acceptance. We need to be an empathic resource to change the legacy that we suffered through so that our children can know they don't have to suffer violation to get their needs met.

## EMPATHY IN PARENTING

"Attachment Parenting" is an approach that begins with lots of bonding through comfort and availability. These are sorely missed components in so many of my clients' lives. Parenting with empathy involves the following actions:

- Stop what you are doing, and give your children your full attention.
- No matter what they say, be appreciative. Say, "Thank you for sharing this. It must be difficult to get this out. You are doing a great job. Keep going, please."

- After your child describes her situation—however disorganized it might be—reframe what she is saying into observations such as "That sounds unsettling," "It sounds like you are under a lot of pressure," "It sounds like you were doing what you could to help," or "It sounds like you are not getting what you need from me, and I need to change how I approach this with you."

- Empathize by using statements such as these: "The rules are still the same, but I need to go about this in a way that feels more respectful. I can see how you could feel upset or discounted. I want to change what I am doing so that the rules are given in a way that includes your feelings. I'm glad you've said something. It makes a lot of sense when I hear your perspective."

- Encourage him to think of what needs to happen next with questions such as "What would you like me to do differently?" and "What needs to happen next to make this better?"

- After the talk, let the connection between you and your child "air out" as you move on to conversation about homework, dinner, or friends, for instance.

- Because parents carry so much power, know that it's NEVER too late to take responsibility for your wrongdoing. One time, I asked a forty-year-old client whether it would make a difference if her father apologized in a specific way for his list of wrongdoings. With tears streaming down her face, she said, "It would never be too late. It would just grieve me that he took so long."

Now for the don'ts.

- Don't use subtractive language such as "but," "however," "yet," or "nevertheless." We all know how patronizing this can be. "You make a lot of sense, but . . ." "You look great in that dress, but/however/yet . . ."
- Don't defend your actions. In other words, don't complain or overexplain with statements like "Honey, Mama was really struggling," "There was a lot going on," or "That was just the way I was taught to act." I have said these things and heard them from parents when I have counseled their children who need validation and get excuses instead. Generally speaking, explaining away our reactions goes nowhere and can cost you tons of energy.
- Don't circle back to the issues your children brought up unless they do. Let your children lead in assertive communication because it's their inner experience, not yours.
- Don't ask rhetorical questions such as "Why would you think/feel that?" or "What were you thinking?" Nothing but shame and contempt comes from such statements. They cause children to shut down, leaving you nothing to show for your energy loss but disconnection.

Bonnie Harris, MSEd, has written a well-reviewed book called *Confident Parents, Remarkable Kids*. In it she summarizes the "Basic Needs of a Child":

- Respect: To be respected as much as any other member of the family
- Power: To have a sense of personal power and capability to make something happen

- Acceptance: To be fully and unconditionally accepted for the person he is
- Trust: To be trusted and have the opportunity to trust others
- Belonging: To feel like an important, cared-about member of the family
- Structure: To be given strong and consistent guidelines in order to know what to expect and what is expected of him
- Boundaries: To have healthy boundaries in order to know the difference between the child's and the parent's responsibilities
- Modeling: To have positive, caring models[7]

Princess Warriors, we stand up and fight to protect *ourselves* as well as the *generations to come.* Our children inherit our true belief of what we are worth. If we're not careful, they inherit our shame, our secrets, and our addictions.

If you are not vigilant about this, your children may die to their instincts when caught in the crosswind of your (their parents') conflicting or demanding agendas. It can swallow your child's needs and create doubt that he or she deserves to live a congruent life—a life in which the inside of the child matches the outside.

Our children are equally capable of absorbing and emulating our redemption. Each generation is a hinge that guides the door in the way it will swing. Which way will your door swing—toward liberation or slavery?

If you have hurt your children verbally or physically, you are not alone. If you are unable to get a rein on this, you owe it to yourself and your child to connect the deeper lie to the source: Who brought this darkness into your heart and convinced you, yet again, that you are not good enough? What lies did you agree to? Don't let that liar control you.

Your children love you and want your unconditional acceptance. They want you to look at them and like them. In this equation, you hold the trump card on their security. Please redeem all the pain—convert the pain into places of power—and be the change you desperately needed as a child. Give your children the truth of their lovability and uniqueness. Those gifts are lasting. And, my dear Princess Warrior, the curses die with you.

## THE PRINCESS WARRIOR AS A SPOUSE

There is a phrase I use in therapy with people who are working on their marriage: "Marriage is mostly a friendship where the empathy goes both ways." Empathy skills depend on concern for others, a desire to help others, seeing things from another person's perspective, feeling discomfort when someone else is having a tough time, being truly interested in what other people are experiencing, and listening before offering an opinion. In short, we sense that we have a moral obligation to care for another. Our marriages can be places of deep healing.

Princess Warriors, your dynamic with your spouse is often the most complicated situation to work through. If you are being victimized by your spouse in a cycle of control and power, you will struggle to heal. We must empathize with ourselves and care about whether our healing process can occur in the midst of cruelty suffered in marriage.

There are patterns, or "love styles," originally developed by Milan and Kay Yerkovich, MA, LPC, in their book and workbook *How We Love,* that can evolve from childhood. These patterns develop expectations and defense mechanisms that lead to five problematic love styles:

1. *Avoider:* I don't need anyone.
2. *Pleaser:* I am responsible to maintain the happiness and well-being of others, because conflict and rejection are deadly and to be avoided at all costs.
3. *Vacillator:* My spouse is the problem in my marriage. There is nothing I can do to improve my marriage because my [spouse] won't change. I need my spouse to take away my bad feelings.
4. *Controller:* I have to control and intimidate in order to get what I want.
5. *Victim:* If I tried harder in my relationship, my spouse wouldn't get so angry.[8]

The Yerkoviches explain that a "secure connector" relationship shows acceptance, safety and communication, support and respect, nurture and comfort, individuality and space, and fun and play. These factors underscore the importance of empathic listening, a resolve to change, an honest inventory of your effect on the other person, support for each other, and hours of mending and tending to the trust and peace of the relationship. We don't usually enter into marriage healed and whole, even if we have done a lot of work on ourselves.

I would advise you to call upon a therapist, mentor couple, and intercessory prayer warriors to support and counsel you in the intimate journey of marriage. From years of working with many couples, I have seen that Satan's devices are alive and well, and they go undetected in a marriage relationship much more often than in other settings.

## LEARN THE TRUTH ABOUT YOURSELF

Love requires grit to reject the lies of our adversary and keep marching forward. It's important that you develop an accurate understanding of where you are strong and capable. Is it in being hospitable, listening, showing love in art, managing people, accounting, practical home-making, or taking care of the elderly, small children, or teens? Do you prefer working behind the scenes as you support another person's visionary style or project? Are you better at leading? Are you moti-vated by awards or rewards that are tangible and public? Or are you more interested in working for personal, quiet exchanges between you and another person? Do you find that you operate better when life is methodical and planned, or when you have the opportunity to improvise?

Now is the time to learn about yourself by talking with other people. Ask those around you how they experience you. Ask what they see as difficulties and blessings in knowing you. What do they see as your strengths and weaknesses? Use the input as a helpful guide as you maximize your strengths, not as an excuse to filter out the affirmations and concentrate instead on the criticism. But learn from both. Ask for support in your weaker areas by visiting with a therapist or life coach. Wise people are teachable and open to feedback when it comes from those they trust. Remember, the people who sought Jesus were re-claimed, redeemed, and restored. We risk becoming isolated, lonely, and emotionally dead without interaction with the truth of who we are—no matter how difficult this is.

If we are not good at something, we need a team. Our weak-nesses can bring out the strengths in others, and on goes the cycle of blessing—not cursing, and certainly not contempt. This is why vulnerability and openness are fundamental to a life fully lived. You, Princess Warrior, were formed for *this*.

## REST AND RESPLENDENCE

One of my favorite words is *shalom*. It is the Hebrew word that means "peace, safety, wellness, happiness, great health, prosperity, harmony, favor, rest and completeness; nothing missing; nothing broken."

*Shalom* describes the state of being that we all seek. It describes a person who has come to Jesus for healing and restoration. *Yeshua,* the Hebrew for "Jesus," is called *Sar shalom,* "Prince of Peace."⁹ His peace is *shalom*.

*Shalom* describes you and me as we do the hard work of rejecting the deceptions of Satan and instead live in God's truth about ourselves, others, life, and the world. Write down the meaning of *shalom,* and put it on your mirror, in your car, in your workspace, in your children's rooms. On the days when things are hanging by a thread, write *shalom* on your hands. You are precious to God as the one and only girl that he made to be just like you.

One marker of those who follow Jesus, I believe, is that they carry *shalom*. Ask God right now for *shalom* to fill you, all whom you love, and all that you love. His *shalom* is the fulfillment of our design. Resting in the battle is only possible in God, the Hero of humanity.

"*In repentance and rest is your salvation, in quietness and trust is your strength. . . .* The LORD longs to be gracious to you; therefore he will rise up to show you compassion. For the LORD is a God of justice.

Blessed are all who wait for him!" (Isaiah 30:15, 18). Your achievements, intelligence, and drive will not save you. And your accomplishments, successes, and awards are not your legacy. My salvation, and yours, is found in rest and repentance.

How often do we hear that we are strengthened by growing quiet and leaning into God's strength as we trust in him? Most magazine articles and self-help books insist that it's up to me. I have included much in this book that is designed to give you practices, exercises, and guidance in moving forward and living in God as a Princess Warrior. But even if you were able to integrate every idea in this book and other wonderful practices to help you heal, it is always the *shalom* of God that feeds you in quiet and rest. God is more powerful by far than our devotion to hard work, self-improvement, and overcoming the past.

Plans are great as a guide, but God heals you with his presence, his lordship, his mercy and restoration. I can't count the number of times I have prayed this prayer, based on 2 Corinthians 5:16–17: *"Be my* shalom. *Be my healer. Give me the senses to feel you. Restore those sandpapered parts of my life where, worn to the bone, there is nothing left. I know you can heal me. In you, through your death and resurrection, all things can become new. By your Spirit, I am made new. Amen."*

I encourage you to lay down this book and do just that. Close your eyes, hear your heart beat, breathe, and say this prayer. Build this into your life. Maybe you will say it at the end of every prayer. Maybe you will pray it over your children. You could say to your children, "I am praying for you. Know that God's *shalom* is with you. I will be praying God's *shalom* over you and in you."

God is indeed our Ruler, our Rest Giver, the Source of our *shalom,* and thus our resplendence. *Resplendent* is a word that encapsulates a great, stunning quality. If we're not shining, brilliant, and gorgeous from within, what have we changed? How are we going to have an impact without this light emanating from us?

## LAST BATTLE

I have given this social ill and personal tragedy of sexual trauma the name Last Battle because it remains a destructive force that cuts through every nation, without regard for religion, race, or creed. It has violated the sanctity of every woman in every decade from ancient times to modern-day news stories. It pierces the heart of every neighborhood, whether urban, suburban, or countryside. It has been an unrelenting and often silent killer. Together we can defeat the Enemy who started this battle that plagues God's handiwork and royal family. And we can reidentify those who have survived this battle for who they really are, Princess Warriors.

Do you know that I just love you? I really do. How do you get out of bed and read this book? I am simply in awe of you. How am I so fortunate as to have your attention—against all that demands your allegiance and focus? I feel like I have been writing to the truly great through all of these pages. The truly good. You have reached for this book with wounded hands, burning eyes, and a heart faint with grief and pain. I have the *utmost* respect for you. Your tenacity and intelligence to stand back from the daily agony of connecting with this betrayal—that achieves its destruction in everything we hold sacred—and seek answers to timeless questions confirms for me what I have

known for years: Satan is vastly intimidated by you. I am just fortunate enough to understand this and share the keys to the kingdom.
You were singled out because of your worth, not despite it. *Never* forget that. Write it on every mirror in your house, until you feel it tat-
tooed on your subconscious.

Now we will turn to our presence in the world and our pursuit of becoming the change we want to see in the world.

## Chapter 14

# HELP FOR THOSE WHO HELP THE OVERCOMERS

> We are each other's harvest; we are each other's
> business; we are each other's magnitude and bond.
>
> —GWENDOLYN BROOKS

Recently, I was sharing with a dear friend the rejection I had felt through certain segments of my life and the isolation I felt in the midst of it, and she said, "I just want to crawl across this table and hold you." My whole body cried, "This is what love is!" I didn't need trite phrases or reasons. I needed that vulnerable and engaged show of presence. Princess Warriors have to have that to heal.

When my clients tell me they were sexually abused, they comment less on the original breach of trust than on the way very few people—even those close to them—seem to care. They seek my time and attention because otherwise they encounter little to no respect or even an attempt to understand what they are experiencing. The community of love, service, and devotion is integral to the Princess Warrior who courageously faces the truth and impact of the insidious pain of sexual violation.

People too often assess the survivor's need for support based on the "severity" of the abuse, how long ago it happened, and whether they believe the survivor "really tried" to help herself. These sorts of responses send the message that the abuse by the perpetrator was only the beginning of the problem.

When a Princess Warrior becomes aware of what has happened to her, an insidious and debilitating shame can overwhelm her. Honor the courage it takes to uncover this reality. Be kind and listen. Don't shy away.

For the survivor, everything has reversed course. The bloodied, dirty bandages are off and the wound is exposed. However, these same Princess Warriors often are asked to go back to life as usual. The Princess Warrior starts to realize why she's always hurt in various places, as she examines her wounds. She is in shock and often needs more care than she will know how to request. This is where you come in. You are someone who can help in tangible, supportive, life-giving ways. You don't have to be an expert, but you do need to be willing to learn a few basic approaches. In this chapter we will look at ways you can help if you are the husband, the parent, the pastor, or the counselor of a Princess Warrior.

## If You Are the Husband

If you are the husband of a survivor, yours is a complex and intricate fight. You are entrusted to be God's emissary of safety and love in the inner sanctum of her deepest fear and terror. Your fight is Special Forces caliber. The rest of us are foot soldiers—worthy and respectable, but definitely not as near the Enemy as you will be. You occupy the place where the greatest rescue can happen. Your role requires grit and raw courage.

Learn what your wife's injury is. Fully understand the unique nature of how ongoing or systematic abuse and sexual violation master the will and intelligence of a person. While God, in his grace, has created our brains with a neuroplasticity that allows us to grow past our violations, you will be the most powerful element of her neuroplastic growth. You can help regenerate neuropathways and re-create cellular integrity in your wife's brain, which will help her body relearn to engage in the need for sexual intimacy born of safe connection. Your love and constancy can disprove her belief that she is bonding with you in fear.

It is all about taking initiative. Initiate a date by saying, "I want to take you out next weekend, and I have everything planned." This includes calling the baby-sitter, making reservations, and planning extras, such as a fancy dessert or drink bar, or a walk around the park. The biggest piece you offer is companionship without conditions. She doesn't have to be dressed up for you.

You cannot remain passive, waiting for your wife to grow toward you. This very often is the tactic I see in my counseling office, and it just reinjures the Princess Warrior. The husband often believes that the best medicine is to let his wife call all of the shots and to give her the power to make most of the decisions about the household to help her regain a voice. (I am not against this, but that is better done in something I describe later as the "summit" in the bulleted list in the next section.)

Decide now that you will not avoid hard situations. Running away when things get hard is one response to being unable to fight the perpetrator. You have every right to feel this way, but you must communicate what you are experiencing to someone.

No one expects you to be a mind reader or an expert in sexual abuse and assault-based trauma. So seek the support of a professional, and reread this book for background information and helpful practices.

Make a list of questions that will help your wife speak to you about how she is doing or how she interprets her process. Also, write down questions about what you read. It is normal not to understand the pain of another person. Sometimes you need to do some research to learn more.

## *Cherishing Your Wife*

Make a separate list of ideas of ways to cherish your Princess Warrior. Here is a list of suggestions to help you get started:

- Identify her love language, as described by Gary Chapman in the book *The Five Love Languages*. (A quick summary: they are nonsexual touch, quality time, gifts, acts of service, and words of affirmation.)
- Talk about her love language and some ways you plan to use her love language more frequently.
- Make a way to celebrate your anniversary with surprises or plans, whatever feels more suitable and enjoyable to you both. Consider also a small celebration of the day of the month, every month, to commemorate your anniversary. This lets your wife know you are thinking of her and that you are glad the two of you got together. This can be done with a phone call or a text.

- Celebrate birthdays with intention and flair—but expense is rarely necessary. Take a day off of work and do something both of you enjoy. Go to a movie, an arcade, a restaurant, or take a walk in the park or go on a bike ride. Some people do countdown gifts; for example, the week before a birthday, they leave daily notes, cards, and small gifts in secluded but findable places.

- Make time to sit and reflect on the week. Ask about highlights or how counseling is going, and tell her about your experience in all of this. Marriage is a mutual friendship in which the empathy goes both ways. It is inevitable that it will be hard for her to hear you, but I challenge Princess Warriors to be empathic because it's good for them. It's a part of the healing process.

- Rub her shoulders, ears, or feet while you talk. Many of the Princess Warriors I have worked with have surprised me with their need for nonsexual touch. They need me to sit close to them with one arm over their shoulder while we discuss certain memories or disappointments. Comfort is different for everyone, so ask your wife what feels safe. Sometimes as memories emerge, what felt safe a month before is no longer welcome.

- Hire a photographer to take pictures of your family; you and your wife; or your wife with the children, grandchildren, pets, and other family members. Some Princess Warriors are artisans and may want their creations to be photographed. Do this in your home, since a home has roots and history, and it's yours.

- Hold an annual picture-viewing date. This means going through your pictures taken over the last year and talking about what the memories were like for each of you.
- Take her to a coffee shop. Bring out some index cards and ask her questions that are written on the cards, such as "What would you do with a lottery win?" "Where have you always wanted to travel?" "Who were your best friends growing up?" "What is your favorite holiday?" "What sort of food comforts you the most?" "What is your favorite time of the week?" "What is your favorite exercise or way to calm down?" "Where do you want to be a year from now?" "What are your dreams as a mother?" "What are your dreams as a grandmother or aunt?" "Where do you want to take your career?" "What would make you feel more financially secure?" "What accomplishments are you most proud of?" "Whom do you consider your allies?" "What relationships create the most distress for you?" and "What about your violation hurts the most right now?" (John Gottman, PhD, has written a helpful guide for conversation prompts in chapter 3 of his book *The Seven Principles for Making Marriage Work*.) Write down your wife's answers on the note cards, and revisit these answers every year. See whether her answers have changed or whether she has reached certain goals.
- Develop a mission statement for your coupleship. For example: "We love through respect and vow to remain students of each other as the years progress. We accept

Christ as the head of our household and vow to remain diligent in our pursuit of his personhood and character. We understand and hold inviolable the importance of voice and honor as a method to remain transparent in all our dealings . . ."

- Hold a monthly summit meeting where you discuss certain functional categories, such as finances, parenting, schedules, recreation, communication methods, affection, in-laws, faith practices, and miscellaneous issues such as pets, neighbors, and community involvement.

- Discuss sexual fulfillment and safety. Determine with your Princess Warrior what sexual safety looks like or would mean to her. Discuss ways to make it safer by making suggestions, such as having it planned, or communicate that certain elements have appeared unsafe for her. Discuss what needs to be avoided so she will feel safe.

- Refer to the introduction for scriptures that identify her worth, and write them on notes that you send her in a card, or via a text or an e-mail.

We need to major in the positives and minor in the negatives, but this does not mean we should avoid the negatives. In my counseling with parents and couples, I call this the 80/20 principle. The majority of your investment is in development of what is safe and encouraging. In other words, notice what is good and noble, and encourage her strengths 80 percent of the time. During the other 20 percent, carefully discuss what is missing, what is needed, or what she does or says that hurts you. Then discuss what you need in order to see the relationship progress and to assist in meeting your needs.

Lastly, do some research together that will show you both that you are bigger than yourselves. You are more resilient in the face of challenges than you think you are. The way to reach this higher level of confidence and self-understanding is to learn what your parents and ancestors stood for. Gather your family history and hers. Find out where generations of your family were born; where they lived and went to school; what they accomplished; and how they prevailed in the face of war, poverty, setbacks, and loss. Discuss traditions and strengths of family members. Research indicates the richer our understanding of our origins, the stronger our self-concept.[1] We are so much more than the difficult pieces of the violation we have endured.

## How to Show Empathy

I'll use my husband, who has also been my best friend these past fifteen years, as an example. He loved me more than he loved what he got from me, and that showed up in the way he validated me. Sometimes my fear and pain would grip me so greatly I was unable to move. I couldn't stop crying for hours at a time. He had never seen someone in the grips of betrayal and loss, but he gave me love, comforted me, and asked very little of me. I, in turn, hope to spend the rest of my days making sure he knows that those actions saved me.

He showed me validation in the way he did not judge me. He never tried to talk me out of how I felt. He simply said, "That makes a lot of sense. I want to help. I want to do _____ for you. Would that help?" Sometimes he nailed it. He just knew. He prays for wisdom. If he didn't get it right, it was my responsibility to suggest something else. He didn't have to be a mind reader; he just needed to show that he wanted to do something.

In the times I have confronted him, he never defended himself by saying, "Well, I see how you struggle with me because your relative/ professor/ex-husband/other men did _____ to you." This may sound logical, but it shames a Princess Warrior and denies her the right to be hurt by you. He has nearly always said, "I'm sorry. I didn't mean to leave you feeling like that. I need to change that in me." He didn't rescue me, nor did he protect me from his problems. But he took responsibility without challenging me.

There have been times I reacted defensively, and his patience has been one of the most healing overtures in our marriage. He didn't withdraw into stony silence. He just looked at me and said, "That is not okay, and that needs to change." He has rights, and he is God's handiwork. I have no right to hurt him, and we must not hurt as we have been hurt. When we do that, the curse just continues and we become what we despised in our perpetrators. We are bigger and mightier than our pain, so we need to act like it.

## Grief Requires Time

Be patient and understanding; your wife will get better with time. Understand that she may need to talk about the traumatic events a great deal before her symptoms lessen. Remember that sexual violation is deeply shaming and overwhelming because there is so much silence laced in the midst of it. Avoid telling your wife that she's being negative and rehashing too much.

Try to anticipate and prepare for dates, situations, places, and events that can trigger a posttraumatic stress disorder (PTSD) reaction. Common triggers include people, places, smells, images, and anniversary dates associated with the trauma. Being protective will bring her great relief because it shows empathy and advocacy—two things that were missing in the past.

Don't take symptoms of PTSD personally. This is particularly difficult because among the symptoms are emotional numbness, anger, and withdrawal. If your Princess Warrior seems distant, irritable, or closed off, remember that she likely needs comfort, not adages. Say little and instead do what you know has helped her feel better. My husband would say, "Let's watch a movie, and I'll rub your feet." It didn't solve the problem, but his caregiving would bolster me to integrate the here and now much more easily.

Don't pressure your loved one into talking about the abuse. For some, talking can be triggering. Let her know you are willing to hear her when she is ready.

## IF YOU ARE THE PARENT OF A PRINCESS WARRIOR

The stunned horror many parents feel when they learn that their child was sexually violated can be the toughest emotion they have to overcome. I have interviewed numerous parents who need their own support. But, instead, people in their community have treated them with suspicion, especially if the violation took place at the hands of a father or a brother.

If such violation occurred within your family, make every effort to end all contact with the perpetrator, and call the authorities to report the crime, no matter how long ago the incident occurred. Notify others within the family that the person violated your child so they can talk to their children about possibly having been violated. If this was done by someone outside of the family system, the same response holds true.

Here are things you can do and pray about doing for your daughter:

- Share with your daughter your outrage over what has happened, and strongly support her battle to heal.
- Never challenge the veracity of her claims.
- Never ask her to reconcile with the family member in question.
- Never talk about how you are torn by your loyalties.
- While you may feel self-doubt and self-blame, stay focused on supporting the services she may need, such as finding a psychiatrist or a naturopath, meeting with a therapist, going through a rape kit at the hospital if the violation just occurred, and other therapies that may be needed to help with addiction to drugs or alcohol, eating disorders, and so forth.
- Do not share her story with anyone she has not given you permission to tell.
- Talk about ways to keep her safe, and then ask what would help.
- Don't ask her for more information than she has already given. But make it clear that you are available to hear her story any time, no matter what.
- Be humbly apologetic for not knowing what was happening to her. Understand that there were clues you probably missed—and she likely knows you missed them. Just own that without being defensive.

On a broader scale, understand that your daughter's tragedy deepens the reality of the battle: "For our struggle is not against flesh and blood, but against the rulers, against the authorities, against the powers of this dark world" (Ephesians 6:12). Get familiar with the Prayer for Declaration of Independence and the Breaking of Curses in chapter 7. As noted previously, read these aloud.

Your power over her healing never ends, and it's *never too late* to do this. Use the scriptures provided at the end of this book's introduction to stake your claim over your child. Send her the verses in texts and cards, and post them on her mirror. Jesus gave his followers the Holy Spirit, the source of his power, and advised them to keep close to him. He said, "All authority in heaven and on earth has been given to me" (Matthew 28:18). But he further encouraged them when he shared that he gave them his authority: "I saw Satan fall like lightning from heaven. I have given you authority to trample on snakes and scorpions and to overcome all the power of the enemy" (Luke 10:18–19).

Many of the practical ideas included in chapter 13 are useful to the parent of a Princess Warrior. Also check the advice given to husbands earlier in this chapter.

You are not asked to rescue your daughter or to seek revenge against her abuser. The main way you can help is to contribute to her feeling safe enough to heal.

## CONSIDERATIONS FOR THE CHURCH

Boz Tchividjian, a former prosecutor and the executive director of GRACE (Godly Response to Abuse in the Christian Environment), helped put together a statement regarding Christian faith and its cover-up of sexual abuse. The statement was released by the American Association of Christian Counselors in 2013. (I have reformatted the statement from a paragraph into bullet points.)

We must face the truths of our own teachings:

- To be a shepherd in the body of Christ and blind to the knowledge that your sheep are being abused by wolves in your midst is to be an inattentive shepherd.
- To judge merely by outward appearances is a failure of righteousness.
- To fail to obey the laws of the land as Scripture commands by declining to report and expose abuse is to be a disobedient shepherd.
- To be told that wolves are devouring our lambs and fail to protect those lambs is to be a shepherd who sides with the wolves who hinder those same little ones from coming to Jesus.
- To fail to grasp the massive web of deception entangling an abuser and set him or her loose among the sheep is to be naïve about the very nature and power of sin.
- To be told a child is being or has been abused and to make excuses for failing to act is a diabolical misrepresentation of God.
- To know a woman is being raped or battered in hidden places and silence her or send her back is to align with those who live as enemies of our God.

- Protecting an institution or organization rather than a living, breathing lamb is to love ministry more than God and to value a human name or institution more than the peerless name of Jesus. . . .

We will "eliminate harmful beasts from the land, make places of blessing for the sheep, deliver them from their enslavers and make them secure in places where no one will make them afraid" (Ezekiel 34:25–28).[2]

Jesus said in describing anyone who would harm "one of these little ones" that it would be better for the abuser to have a millstone tied around his neck and be thrown into the sea (see Mark 9:42). Jesus will never condone protecting the abuser at the expense of the abused.

Even our judicial system recognizes accomplices as complicit in the egregious act or crime. Do you want to be complicit in this terrible personal and social crime? Then stand up. Ask God for courage to live as an advocate, a strong man or woman taking upon yourself this fight for the survivor's personal rights and freedoms.

If someone reports that he or she has been sexually abused, call authorities: police, child protection services, and other trusted adults in the community. Gather names of recommended therapists, and begin the hunt for the advice you need to nurture, comfort, and support this person. A gospel-centered response to child sexual abuse and the sexual violation of anyone at any age begins with understanding that silence is not an option.

### Putting an End to Blaming the Victim

The data prove that, according to conservative estimates, at least one in ten children is sexually abused.

Christian leaders, pastors, teachers, and youth-group workers need to do their part to help girls and young women take care of themselves as individuals and within a romantic context. Teach them how to set boundaries and avoid getting into situations that would overwhelm them. Give them the tools to gain a sense of individuality and meaning in the world at large, especially as a princess in the royal family of God. Refer to the protection steps on my website at LastBattle.org.

Let girls and young women know they can count on your support and guidance if they are dealing with any choices they regret. Never, ever, ever tell them that their worth rides on their sexual behavior or past history. You don't know if you are talking to a young woman who has been sexually abused. And I don't think I have to reiterate how counter to the gospel it is for us to blame the victim.

## IF YOU ARE A THERAPIST

Dr. Diane Langberg created a list of how a therapist can stand with a Princess Warrior.[3] I have summarized her list:

1. Therapists must acknowledge their own inadequacies. We cannot make it better. We don't have the solution, but we are called to be there and to love.
2. The healing process can be long, so we need to persevere even when we are not "wanted." We must be inviting and affirming, but not pushy.
3. We are in a spiritual battle. We must stand against "the spiritual forces of evil" on the survivor's behalf.
4. God gives us faith in what he can do—not in our own powers, but in his. The discernment required for work

with this population must be Spirit-led. Pray before,
during, and after the session that God is carrying her in
his loving arms.

5. As therapists, we are called to be in the pain, but we must
protect ourselves by reiterating and calling upon the truth:
"Greater is he who is in you than he who is in the world."

We are often holding faith for clients, believing for them what
they cannot believe—that they are made for a future full of hope and
strength. Remember that the healing of the Princess Warrior is ultimately hers to choose. You are an emissary to respond the way God
would have you respond, but you are a stand-in for the real thing—the
work of the Spirit in the lives of these precious survivors.

Respect them and know that it's less what you say and more what
you do. Abuse victims hear your words, but they mostly gauge the
spirit and intention of your behavior. If you are calm and compassionate, what you say will be secondary to your client's ability to trust your
intentions. Come off controlling or judgmental, impatient or domi-
neering, and you will likely lose her altogether.

## Chapter 15

# FIGHTING ALONGSIDE THE PRINCESS WARRIOR

Like dawn spreading across the mountains
a large and mighty army comes,
such as never was in ancient times
nor ever will be in ages to come.

—JOEL 2:2

When a community is a safe place, a Princess Warrior regains momentum and a sense of having a future. Her community becomes a battle-free place in which she can exercise her rights and privileges as an equal member. No matter what created your injury or mine, we are designed to heal *with* people. If we are injured by people, we can heal with people. We can feel the truth and freedom God has for us in *connection*. We are designed to be restored in connection.

When victims are believed, they begin to know that their pain is part of their story but not the core of who they are. But in the absence of the understanding of other people, the survivor is likely to dam the flow of what she feels. Instead of sharing the process of healing with others, she survives on the empty calories of addictive work styles, religiosity, perfectionism, promiscuity, chemical addiction, and other escapist activity. She also may suffer physical symptoms that are difficult to diagnose.

We need the expertise of knowledgeable therapists as well as the compassion and safety of everyday people. We need law enforcement and attorneys to speak up for us. We need pastors and clergy to share the pain with us and educate their congregants about the prevalence and perniciousness of this reality. We need teachers and doctors to report the crimes. We need relatives and those in our personal communities to stand by the oppressed sister, cousin, grandchild, or child and to fight for her with their resources—practical, financial, and spiritual.

This is not a problem that only some of us should care about. If you heard that one in three people would experience before their eighteenth birthday something that would leave them in a nearly fatal condition, you would speak out against the cause of such destruction. If taking a prescription drug or driving a certain automobile or eating a type of food presented that much of a threat, you would join with others in calling attention to the threat and demanding that corrective action be taken.

So why is so little being done to help protect our children from the threat of sexual violation? And what does prevention look like? Along with many others, I have been trained by Darkness to Light (D2L), a nonprofit organization aimed at the *prevention* of sexual abuse among the eighteen-and-younger population. Posted on our website, Last Battle.org, is the prevention training module along with ways to become educated and get involved in the solution.

## Warnings: What Not to Do

We must accept that we are not able to supply answers to the problem of pain. Dan Allender has written that "Christians seem to despise reality."[1] This becomes apparent when a girl or woman goes to Christian leaders seeking help after sexual violation. Often, a rationale is presented that protects the perpetrator while the victim is shamed and made to feel that she was responsible for the violation. When I went to Christian leaders after my abuse, I was told that I must have been sinning and made myself a target for sexual harassment. The Christian person who told me this was looking for a way to control the uncontrollable—abusive behavior committed against me by a college professor.

Don't side with the evildoer. There are people who could corroborate the victimization, and yet they take the position that the perpetrator didn't commit the crime, or they believe the person's actions were misinterpreted, or they make excuses for the crimes committed by the perpetrator. In their view, the perpetrator should be forgiven, should be seen for his positive qualities, or is in need of rehabilitation. This is open betrayal of the woman who was violated.

Don't join the voices of betrayal. Rather, join in battle alongside a Princess Warrior, knowing that you might be judged yourself, you might be considered the enemy, and you might lose friends over your decision. Still, take the side of justice and mercy in standing in defense of the Princess Warrior.

First we will talk about what *not* to do and say, followed by what you *can* do to make a positive difference in very practical ways. Here are seven ways that people contribute to the undeserved shame and guilt suffered by those who have been violated:

1. Her perpetrator may be a family member, and people don't want to change schedules and family customs to separate the perpetrator from the survivor.

2. Her family may ask her not to report the crime, saying they will handle the situation within the family. This minimizes the offense and leaves the woman questioning the validity of her pain and—worse—whether she is worth protecting.

3. People may convey that she is making up a story about having been sexually violated, especially if the abuse took place years earlier. Thus there may be pressure to move on so that family and/or friends are not asked to reconstruct reality.

4. People might spiritualize the abuse by saying God has a plan and that it's time to just heal and move on. This sends the message that she is loved and supported only to the degree she complies with the wishes of others.

5. She is presented with reasons why the perpetrator should be forgiven: "He is/was extremely confused and needy, and it's now time to forgive him."

6. People may warn against judging others, saying the woman can't know all that was going on in the heart and mind of the perpetrator. Forgiveness is presented as the antidote to the sin of judging another person.

7. Expressions of anger are called into question, equated with vindictiveness or said to be holding back a woman's progress in moving past the violation. My response is this: "The path to forgiveness becomes a choice *only after* a woman is supported and generously loved *in* her anger." Wrath is a part of God's love. The wrath against sin and abuse that we feel on our own behalf promotes an appropriate love of self.

## WHAT YOU *CAN* DO TO MAKE A DIFFERENCE

You can help undo the devil's work in the life of a Princess Warrior. First, believe in her. Believe in her future and believe her pain, no matter how long ago the original wounds were created. Create a new bond of love and enjoyment, and engage her with your compassion. Compassion means, by definition, to "fellow-feel and suffer for the sufferings."[2] Cry with her. Hold her in the silence and void of what was taken without permission. Never doubt what she says. Never compel her to action or to understand *your* perspective.

As you offer help, you are supporting a soul who must have her basic needs met. She will fight for herself, but this stays more consistent when you fight for her.

Princess Warriors often were taught early on not to ask for their needs to be met. That is why it won't help if you say to her, "Call me if you need anything." It might make you feel better, but the Princess Warrior will not start letting you know every time she could use your help. Instead, take the initiative to be present with her. Ask her when it would be convenient to meet for coffee, go on a walk, have dinner, or do other things together. Write a check to help with expenses, but don't ask how much she "really" needs.

As a Christian community we need to admit our limitations. None of us has all the answers that are needed to help a person. It is uncomfortable not to know why something happened, but it is better to admit that we don't know than to issue a trite phrase, which will offer nothing in the way of help to a hurting Princess Warrior.

Instead, side with her. "I am outraged and hurt that this happened to you. You are amazing for taking this difficult journey. My respect and admiration for you go beyond what I can express. I want to help in any way that makes you know that I am with you and you are safe with me. Here are my ideas. [Provide them.] Would that help you?"

Another way to put it is this: "I am stepping up for you in any way that feels safe and respectful. I have the following ideas and want to run them by you. [Share them.] Would any of these help? Are you comfortable if I share this with anyone who might also be able to step up with me?"

Ask permission to act, then offer what you can, whether it's a weekly text with an encouraging statement or a small gift you place on her doorstep. But be very careful when sharing scripture. Some scripture makes a Princess Warrior cringe, such as "In all things God works for the good of those who love him" (Romans 8:28). Equally upsetting is "Love covers over a multitude of sins" (1 Peter 4:8). The upsetting thing about this type of Bible verse is that the Princess Warrior can infer that she is supposed to be okay or that she is unlovable and has contributed to the lack of justice and loss of love that she already feels.

Be *consistent* about letting her know that you are on her team. Mark it on your calendar to do this weekly, biweekly, monthly— whatever you can do. I urge you not to overpromise and underdeliver. However, you can do something rather than nothing. If you find her favorite chocolates or food item at the store, pick it up and send it with a card. By helping in these ways, you have an opportunity to under- stand the underbelly of the effects of sin on the front lines of battle. God is entrusting you with this.

Honor her need to feel wrath. It is usually not until there is anger—when the deadened nervous system awakens to the reality of the crime of sexual violation—that Princess Warriors begin to heal. Yet other people are prone to label her wrath as sin. The truth is just the opposite. We honor God by honoring who he created us to be. He created us to have a visceral response to violation so that we can be discerning and wise. Wrath is a legitimate response to violation, and it is part of the healing process. What a celebration of triumph God must feel when we say, "I engage my wrath to protect myself and to promote who you have made me to be."

In Isaiah 13, we see God's wrath in connection to his love. "I will punish the world for its evil, the wicked for their sins. I will put an end to the arrogance of the haughty and will humble the pride of the ruth- less. . . . Therefore I will make the heavens tremble; and the earth will shake from its place at the wrath of the LORD Almighty, in the day of his burning anger" (verses 11–13).

Likewise, a Princess Warrior may need to repeat her story, to voice her anger, many times before she can let go of it. Breaking out of si- lence is a long process, especially in cases where her voice has been suppressed for years.

Below are practical ideas to get her to connect her past experience with who she is in the present. This is part of her healing journey in a community context:

- Share with her that you want to make her tea and listen to her, or watch a movie, read poetry, or read Scripture until she falls asleep.

- Let her know that you want to join her in an exercise class, or go for a walk or run. Let her cry if she wants or needs to.

- Make dinner for her and with her.

- Make a collage or dream board with her. In this project, you and she find images in magazines that tell her story and point out who she is beyond the trauma.

- Drive her to counseling and wait in the waiting room, and offer to join her and hold her throughout her counseling session.

- Give her a baseball bat to use to hit pillows and let her scream with primal rage.

- Give her a boxing bag and gloves so she can hit back against all that she suffered.

- Attend a self-defense course with her.

- Sign up for art classes with her so she and you can draw, paint, and sculpt. Many recreation centers offer such classes for a nominal expense.

- Develop a fund to help cover the costs of therapy, legal support, massage treatment, chiropractic care, or medical or nutritional support.

- Do what you can to help her get enough sleep. That
  might include being present in her home overnight if she
  has been feeling unsafe or arranging to have a security
  system installed. Other ideas include reading to her from
  a devotional or inspirational book, bringing a gentle and
  affectionate pet for a visit, or giving her a compact disc or
  a downloadable file of Scripture being read, which she
  can play as she is falling asleep.

## BENEDICTION PRAYER

In doing what you can to reach out to a Princess Warrior with practical acts of support, don't forget prayer. As we discussed earlier, sexual abuse is not just a social problem, a crime, or a symptom of the perpetrator's personality disorder. It is one face of evil that has been unleashed in the world. It is a concerted spiritual and physical attack on the daughters of God, girls and women created in God's image and given the Holy Spirit to do the work of God on earth. Satan targets God's beautiful creations, the coheirs of Christ, for horrible forms of attack. Sexual violation is evidence of Satan's attempts to destroy girls and women.

Do not neglect prayer as a weapon in spiritual warfare. As you come alongside a Princess Warrior, always go to God in prayer. Here is a prayer that calls to mind the love, grace, and power of our God.

Our Father, we thank you for your Son, Jesus Christ, through
whom all things are made. We ask that you grant rivers of

mercy, streams of grace, oak-strong strength, tender nurture, and generous reward for everyone who has read this book—for those who struggle and for those committed to help in the struggle.

Allow us to rise with you in resurrection and to identify with your holy victory. We invite you and your *shalom* into the cells and marrow of our being and ask that your *shalom* would heal all who have chosen to walk this path of truth and healing. We ask you to regenerate the dead places, to heal the wounds, to revive the creativity and passion of every Princess Warrior and every important relationship in their lives.

We especially ask you to guard and protect each woman who has suffered as a result of neglect and abuse. We ask that you dignify their lives with your truth and blessing as they blossom into their true nature, a nature that reflects your handiwork, your attributes, and your promises.

Help us to represent you in your victory as princesses in your holy and royal family.

Thank you for making us equal citizens and warriors on behalf of the truth of who you have designed us to be and the truth of our fight for the millions of women and girls who are among us now and those to come.

I thank you for those who have read this book seeking guidance for ways to bring your restoration to Princess Warriors. Honor them with wisdom, tenacity, and courage as they offer healing, hope, and vision to the Princess Warrior(s) in their lives.

Grant all Princess Warriors and all who care for them rest and resplendence.

We pray this knowing you are "able to do immeasurably more than all we ask or imagine, according to [your] power that is at work within us" (Ephesians 3:20).

Amen.

Thank you for the high honor of addressing you, Princess Warriors—a worthy and beloved population, indeed. Thank you, supporters and friends, for reading this text and learning how to join the truth and lend comfort and respect to those who have been struck by this terrible evil.

Princess Warriors, when we agree that what happened to us occurred at the hands of those who envy our kindness, strength, and purity of heart, we can start to perceive that our battle against darkness is because of our light, not despite it. It is not personal to each of us; it's genocide of the searing beauty of the female soul. It is an attempt to kill our hearts and voice, to rot us from the inside, insidiously and nearly imperceptibly. There are really no other explanations. Women are meant to knead the world into a place that attaches value, strength, and hope to all that God has created—things that are foundational and creative so that the world can inspire God's "kingdom come, [his] will be done" (Matthew 6:10).

And let this also be a warning to you who do not see what battle we wage, who turn away, becoming complicit in this ever-darkening hour. "Woe to those who call evil good and good evil, who put darkness for light and light for darkness" (Isaiah 5:20). Woe to you because

God's kingdom is waking up. We will not turn away and join the shaming and oppressive silence. Not for one more day. For every one of you who seeks to intimidate and deceive, there are a thousand of us who see you and will call you out.

We wake up, Princess Warriors, and reclaim our royal birthright to move From Pain to Power. You will never, ever stand alone again. Semper Fi.

*Appendix A*

# YOU ARE FAR FROM ALONE

My internist mentioned that half of her female patients have been sexually violated. The reality is that every 107 seconds, somewhere in America, someone is sexually assaulted, thus the statistics of this silent and growing majority.[1]

As we have noted, today's working statistic is that one in four girls will be sexually assaulted before her eighteenth birthday, and that one in three women will be sexually assaulted in her lifetime. Consider, in a projective analysis, those you know who have been raped after they were married (including some by their husbands) or those who have experienced date rape. Now consider how few of these women reported the violation to any authorities, especially if they were a child when it happened. I think it's safe to estimate that the statistics would start to climb if we were to add these figures to the data.

In fact, according to the National Sexual Violence Resource Center website, "Statistics About Sexual Violence," rape is the most underreported crime; 63 percent of sexual assaults are not reported to police.[2] Just as troubling is the fact that sexual violation frequently is covered up, even when the victim attempts to report it. Survivors are blamed for what happened, they are shamed into feeling that they brought on the violation, or they are promised justice that never comes about. The survivor is penalized for having the courage to report the abuse. Female members of the military, for instance, who reported instances of sexual violation have been charged with adultery, fined, demoted in rank, and humiliated. Other institutions—from colleges to corporations to religious institutions—likewise are known to downplay the seriousness of sexual violation or to quietly push incidents aside in the interest of preserving the organization's reputation.

Of those who report, the prevalence of false reporting is between 2 percent and 10 percent, according to several studies conducted in 2006, 2009, and 2010.[3]

Another often-neglected issue is that of intimate partner rape. In 2002, a researcher found that in current relationships of 1,108 US residents, 34 percent of married women reported incidents of unwanted sex with their husbands.[4] Also, at least 14 percent of married women were physically threatened with force by their husbands to have sexual intercourse.[5]

It was also discovered that marital rape is the most common form of rape, and it was found to occur at twice the rate of stranger rape. More than one in every seven women who has ever been married was raped during marriage, and 40 to 50 percent of women who are battered experience intimate partner rape.[6]

On June 20, 2013, the World Health Organization reported the results of its first-ever systematic study of the prevalence of violence against women globally, by both partners and nonpartners. Some 35 percent of all women will experience either intimate partner violence or nonpartner sexual violence. This same study showed that intimate partner violence is the most common type of violence against women, affecting 30 percent of women worldwide, with the highest prevalence in Africa, the Eastern Mediterranean area, and Southeast Asia. In the Americas, the rate stands at almost 30 percent.[7]

Because of the myth that marital rape is less traumatic than rape committed by a stranger or acquaintance, the legal system views intimate partner rape as a less serious crime. Victims of such abuse are less likely to be believed. In fact, offenders in cases of intimate partner rape regularly are allowed access to survivors as a result of shared responsibility for childrearing and asset management. Because of this, survivors may experience longer-lasting trauma, higher levels of physical injury, higher incidence of multiple rapes, advice from others to "put up with" rape, and difficulty defending themselves against future acts of sexual assault.[8]

## LACK OF SAFETY IN COMMUNITIES THAT SHOULD BE SAFE

The church in America—both Catholic and Protestant—is caught in the web of sex crime. Justice for victims of sexual violation in the church is far from assured. Boz Tchividjian is a former child abuse prosecutor, who now advocates for children hurt by sexual abuse of any kind in Christian environments.[9] Tchividjian says that more than two-thirds of prosecuting attorneys involved in cases of sexual abuse of children in a church setting report that pastors have gotten involved "in a *supportive role* only for the accused perpetrator, not the alleged victim."[10]

Whether such pastors do this out of ignorance or intentionally is not known. But it demonstrates how blind we are to the work of the devil in children's lives and the lives of so many victims of sexual violation.

Religion that emphasizes rules, loyalty, and obedience has the effect of teaching victims to stay quiet in the name of Jesus—or at least in the name of protecting his reputation. However, Jesus has nothing to do with this. It's just sick people finding another way to hurt vulnerable people, namely women and children, in a setting that should be completely safe.

Even in a setting where attempts are made to silence the victim, know that she has power that intimidates Satan. We can derive strength in the places that were broken because of this passage:

> For he chose us in him before the creation of the world to be
> holy and blameless in his sight. In love he predestined us for
> adoption [as his daughters] through Jesus Christ, in accordance
> with his pleasure and will—to the praise of his glorious grace,
> which he has freely given us in the One he loves [Jesus]. In him
> we have redemption through his blood, the forgiveness of sins,
> in accordance with the riches of God's grace that he lavished
> on us. With all wisdom and understanding he made known to
> us the mystery of his will according to his good pleasure, which
> he purposed in Christ, to be put into effect when the times
> reach their fulfillment. (Ephesians 1:4–10)

Who but the devil, the one never invited into this glory and lavish grace, would want to make sure we don't know about our inheritance? Because Paul, who wrote Ephesians, goes on to say that we are (as believers) "marked in him with a seal, the promised Holy Spirit, who is a deposit guaranteeing our inheritance until the redemption of those who are God's possession—to the praise of his glory" (verses 13–14).

# POSTTRAUMATIC STRESS DISORDER, THE WOUNDED BRAIN

Posttraumatic stress disorder (PTSD) is a normal reaction to undue and deadly stress. Considering that we were essentially made for the Garden of Eden, our systems can be short-circuited when circumstances deliver too many serious threats. You and I were not designed to suffer. Our brains have a default mode for duress, but not *prolonged* duress.

PTSD is not an illness but an injury to the brain. My clinical experience has shown that many secondary mental health disorders can be linked to trauma. Those disorders include bipolar II disorder, severe anxiety, phobias, severe depression, and obsessive-compulsive disorder. These disorders can result from a single life-threatening event or an accumulation of incidents.

Children are especially vulnerable to PTSD if they witness or are victimized by verbal, physical, or sexual abuse, or by regular intrusion and violation of their physical or psychological space. The violation might include sexual assault, bullying, stalking, harassment, and domestic violence. The extent to which the traumatic event was un-expected, uncontrollable, and inescapable also plays a role.

Signs and symptoms of PTSD can arise suddenly, arise gradually, or come and go over time. They can be triggered by something that reminds the sufferer of the original traumatic event such as noise, an image, certain words, or a smell. While victims experience PTSD differently, there are three main types of symptoms: reexperiencing the traumatic event, avoiding reminders of the trauma, and increased anxiety and emotional arousal.

Reexperiencing a traumatic event may include intrusive, upsetting memories of the event; flashbacks; nightmares; feelings of intense distress when reminded of the trauma; and intense physical reactions to reminders of the event, such as a pounding heart, rapid breathing, nausea, muscle tension, sweating, and headaches. Avoidance may include staying away from activities, places, thoughts, and feelings that remind the victim of the trauma; an inability to remember important aspects of the trauma; a loss of interest in activities or life in general; feelings of detachment from others; emotional numbness; or a sense of a limited future. Increased anxiety and emotional arousal may include difficulty falling asleep or staying asleep, irritability or outbursts of anger, difficulty concentrating, being on constant "red alert," or jumpiness and nervousness.[1]

If trauma is prolonged, extreme, or repetitive, it can physically injure the brain. The neuron pathways in the amygdala (the fight-flight-freeze mechanism, near the brainstem) lose their "elasticity" or ability to recover. The liver needs to produce more sugar for energy and the adrenal glands have to supply cortisol, which impairs verbal memory performance among many other brain functions. The body depletes its resources, and systematically, the body's automated responses malfunction. The memory system stays mostly "offline," so trauma events appear as fragmented, disconnected bits of memory. With fragmented memory bits, the memory database has gaps, but the body keeps sensing danger and sending out stress-response signals. There is disruption of short-term memory and the onset of hypervigilance.

While damaging and far from normal behavior and experience, these developments help manage short-term survival and address short-term danger. A person suffering from PTSD "cannot separate 'now and safe' from 'now and danger.' "[2]

The brain experiences emotional responses that are immediate and overwhelming, out of measure with the actual stimulus. An event triggers a much more significant emotional threat. This emotional response can cover the rest of the brain in a millisecond if a threat is perceived. Three signs are common: strong emotional reaction; sudden onset of increased arousal such as hypervigilance, panic, or anger; and post-episode realization that a reaction may have been inappropriate.

The person's body will go into a fight-flight-freeze response, typically occurring without the benefit of logic or reason. A PTSD sufferer can retrain her or his brain to engage logic through self-nurturing and by taking advantage of practical tools to move beyond these symptoms and reactions.

A Princess Warrior needs to know that she is not going crazy; she is simply injured. Her brain is doing what it knows to control pain and minimize exposure to power loss. There are many ways for an abused person to move beyond the panic and sense of loss of control of PTSD. She can regain the power with which the Lord designed her.

The brain suffers at a physical, organic level, producing the effects

I described. Your body may have physically endured the violation, but your mind, will, and emotions also lost command. Those aspects of your being are working overtime to make sure you are never without your control again.

## THE BRAIN CAN HEAL

Your brain can heal. Your body will coordinate with the brain to digest a former trigger as a thing of the past, not a haunting reality that threatens you today. This shift changes your understanding of the traumatic event. You can then begin to separate who you are from the event. You are a whole person and a survivor; you are not defined by the trauma.

Through nurturing activity and therapeutic mind-body practice, your body can begin to refuse the powerlessness it once felt. It can identify the lies that brought on shame and silence. You can now begin to fight the shame messages and reconstruct your brain and your body one neuropathway and one newly created brain cell at a time. Your brain can heal. *Neuroplasticity* or "brain plasticity" refers to changes in neural pathways and synapses that result from changes in behavior, environment, and neural processes as well as changes resulting from bodily injury.

You *can* get back what was taken in sexual violation. The adage that "neurons that fire together wire together" is true. It also is true that when you take back control through intentional self-nurturing practices and mind-body or somatic therapies, the fact that neurons that fire together wire together also *heals* you.

The end result of this journey of feeling and coming back to your senses is that you come to see that all parts of your self are precious and uniquely made with an eternal purpose. The child who was hurt and used, or the young woman who was assaulted and then had to put the pieces back together, becomes the beloved and nurtured Princess Warrior. She speaks, fights, and wants to give back to herself what was taken.

You will be heard by your Maker, who follows your voice till he finds you in the forest of your choices and experiences. But you, dear Princess Warrior, must cry out. You must say, "I don't want to be here! Show me you are here! I want hope and healing! I want my power and design restored to me!"

Those who wake up to their own needs are blessed with answers.

As I write this, I do not pretend to know exactly how you feel, but I write to let you know that you are heroic when you call, "I want out!" Give yourself permission to engage in the choice to heal. You are strong enough to seek truth as you allow doubt, pain, and loneliness to surface.

Ask that the hand of God, made flesh in the Lord Jesus Christ, whose friendship remains in the Holy Spirit, will visit you in your daily life, in your senses, and in the way you think.

*Postscript*

# WAYS TO OBTAIN
# ADDITIONAL HELP

I would enjoy hearing your thoughts about *From Pain to Power*. If you have found insights in the book empowering, hopeful, or challenging, please enter the discussion at LastBattle.org.

I would be glad to speak to your church, organization, or event as my schedule allows. You can contact me at MaryEllenMann@Last Battle.org.

Our website exists to help you and those who stand with you to access the care you need. You will find comments from other Princess Warriors, blog posts, helpful information, and links to supportive legal and therapeutic professionals. Our aim is to create trust as we honor, advocate, and support the journey of healing and begin a legacy in the world at large. Please take a moment to look at what www.lastbattle .org has to offer you.

# Notes

## Introduction: Your Personal Invitation

1. Marilyn Van Derbur, *Miss America by Day* (Denver: Oak Hill Ridge, 2003), 257, italics in the original.

## Chapter 1: I Have Walked Where You Walk

1. Madison Park, "WHO: 1 in 3 Women Experience Physical or Sexual Violence," *CNN,* June 20, 2013, www.cnn.com/2013/06/20/health /global-violence-women/index.html.

2. Statistic from www.parentsformeganslaw.org/public/statistics _childSexualAbuse.html.

3. GNESA (Georgia Network to End Sexual Assault), www.gnesa.org /about-sexual-assault. This statistic is listed on their home page under "Rape Facts," parenthetically noted as a quote from a CDC report in 1994.

4. C. P. Krebs, C. Lindquist, T. Warner, B. Fisher, and S. Martin, "The Campus Sexual Assault (CSA) Study," October 2007. Retrieved from the National Criminal Justice Reference Service: www.ncjrs.gov/pdf files1/grants/221153.pdf.

5. Howard N. Snyder, PhD, "Sexual Assault of Young Children as Reported to Law Enforcement: Victim, Incident, and Offender Characteristics," *National Center for Juvenile Justice,* July 2000, 10, table 6, www.bjs.gov/content/pub/pdf/saycrle.pdf.

6. Oprah Winfrey, quoted in Van Derbur, *Miss America by Day,* 411–12.

7. Dan Allender, *The Wounded Heart: Hope for Adult Victims of Childhood Sexual Abuse* (Colorado Springs: NavPress, 2008), 47–50.

8. Another violation is human trafficking—and it is the greatest scourge of our time. Anyone trapped in sex trafficking is being sexually violated because it is a forced, power-over dynamic that destroys the Princess Warrior's ability to protect her rights and dignity. Being trafficked can happen, however, even in everyday relationships. While money may not be exchanged, there is a notable enslavement that people can suffer in the way that powerlessness permeates the dynamic of victimization.

## Chapter 2: The Warrior's Power and Royal Design

1. John Eldredge and Stasi Eldredge, *Captivating: Unveiling the Mystery of a Woman's Soul,* (Nashville: Thomas Nelson, 2005), 84–85, italics in the original.

2. Eldredge and Eldredge, *Captivating,* 85, italics in the original.

3. Psalm 46:1–3, 5.

4. Snyder, "Sexual Assault of Young Children as Reported to Law Enforcement," 4.

5. Jennifer Truman, Lynn Langton, and Michael Planty, "Criminal Victimization, 2012," US Department of Justice, NCJ 243389, October 2013, www.bjs.gov/content/pub/pdf/cv12.pdf, 2, table 1.

6. Fyodor Dostoevsky, quoted in the epilogue of *The Brothers Karamazov* (New York: Bantam Books, 1970), xiii, italics in the original.

7. Our website, www.lastbattle.org, can be referenced to identify different outreaches regarding this reality.

## Chapter 3: If God Is All-Powerful, Why Were You Abused?

1. Lee Strobel, *The Case for Christ*, DVD (La Mirada, CA: La Mirada Films, 2008).

## Chapter 4: This Is Where You Take Charge

1. Christiane Northrup, *Women's Bodies, Women's Wisdom* (New York: Bantam Books, 2010), 36, 32, italics in the original.

2. "How often does child sexual abuse take place?," The Children's Assessment Center, Houston, Texas. Parenthetically noted as a quote from Smith et al., 2000; Borman-Fulks et al., 2007. www.cachouston.org/child-sexual-abuse-facts/.

3. Kenneth S. Kendler, Cynthia M. Bulik, Judy Silberg, John M. Hettema, John Myers, and Carol A. Prescott, "Childhood Sexual Abuse and Adult Psychiatric and Substance Use Disorders in Women: An Epidemiological and Cotwin Control Analysis," *Archives of General Psychiatry* 57, no. 10 (October 2000): 953–59.

4. Angela Browne and David Finkelhor, "Impact of Child Sexual Abuse: A Review of the Research," *Psychological Bulletin* 99, no. 1 (1986): 66–77; Lauren Book, "Economic and Fiscal Impacts of Child Sexual Abuse in Florida," March 2015, www.miamiherald.com/news/local/community/miami-dade/article13339341.ece/BINARY/Read%20the%20report.pdf.

5. Kendler et al., "Childhood Sexual Abuse."

6. Beth E. Molnar, Stephen L. Buka, and Ronald C. Kessler, "Child Sexual Abuse and Subsequent Psychopathology: Results from the National Comorbidity Survey," *American Journal of Public Health* 91, no. 5 (May 2001): 753–60.

7. Elizabeth M. Saewyc, Lara L. Magee, and Sandra E. Pettingell, "Teenage Pregnancy and Associated Risk Behaviors Among Sexually Abused Adolescents," *Perspectives on Sexual and Reproductive Health* 36, no. 3 (May–June 2004): 98–105.

8. Jennie G. Noll, Chad E. Shenk, and Karen T. Putnam, "Childhood Sexual Abuse and Adolescent Pregnancy: A Meta-Analytic Update," *Journal of Pediatric Psychology* 34, no. 4 (May 2009): 366–78.

9. Sally Zierler, Lisa Feingold, Deborah Laufer, Priscilla Velentgas, Ira Kantrowiz-Gordon, and Kenneth Mayer, "Adult Survivors of Childhood Sexual Abuse and Subsequent Risk of HIV Infection," *American Journal of Public Health* 81, no. 5 (May 1991): 572.

10. "Helping Survivors of Sexual Abuse: Targeting a silent breastfeeding barrier: Child and adult sexual abuse, physical and emotional abuse," North Carolina Breastfeeding Coalition, http://ncbfc.org/wp-content/uploads/2014/04/Sex_Abuse_Survivors_4-10.pdf. Based on the 2005 study by Penny Van Esterik and Karen Wood, "From Hurting Touch to Healing Touch: The Infant Feeding Experiences of Women Survivors of Child Sexual Abuse," in partnership with the National Network on Environments and Women's Health (NNEWH) in Canada.

## Chapter 5: You Are Made by God, and Your Life Is Sacred

1. Based on Edmund J. Bourne, *The Anxiety and Phobia Workbook* (Oakland: New Harbinger, 2000), 283–84.

2. John Eldredge, *Waking the Dead: The Glory of a Heart Fully Alive* (Nashville: Thomas Nelson, 2003), 77, italics in the original.

3. Eldredge and Eldredge, *Captivating*, 195.

4. Henry Cloud and John Townsend, *Boundaries: When to Say Yes, How to Say No to Take Control of Your Life* (Grand Rapids: Zondervan, 1992), 75.

5. Adapted from Glenn Schiraldi, *The Post-Traumatic Stress Sourcebook* (Los Angeles: Lowell House, 2000), 385–86.

6. Roy Baumeister, quoted in Harriet Brown, "The Boom and Bust Ego: The Less You Think About Your Own Self-Esteem, the Healthier You'll Be," *Psychology Today,* January/February 2012, 70–73, www.psychologytoday.com/articles/201112/the-boom-and -bust-ego.

7. Henry Cloud, *Necessary Endings: The Employees, Businesses, and Relationships That All of Us Have to Give Up in Order to Move Forward* (New York: HarperCollins, 2010), 9.

8. Patrick Carnes, *The Betrayal Bond* (Deerfield Beach, FL: Health Communications, 1997), 125–27.

9. Provided in part by Abram Maslov's "Hierarchy of Needs," quoted in Tamara Lowe, *Get Motivated: Overcome Any Obstacle, Achieve Any Goal, and Accelerate Your Success with Motivational DNA* (New York: Doubleday, 2008), 71–72.

10. C. S. Lewis, *Mere Christianity* (New York: Simon and Schuster, 1976), 205.

## Chapter 6: Preparing for Battle

1. Eldredge, *Waking the Dead,* 47.

2. Brené Brown, TED Talk, "The Power of Vulnerability," filmed June 20, 2010, www.ted.com/talks/brene_brown_on_vulnerability /transcript?language=en.

3. Timothy Keller, "Spiritual Warfare," *Gospel in Life,* January 29, 2012, http://sermons2.redeemer.com/sermons/spiritual-warfare.

4. Public domain.

## Chapter 8: Reconstructing Your Mind and Emotions

1. Eldredge, *Waking the Dead,* 40.

## Chapter 10: What to Do When You Doubt God

1. Cloud and Townsend, *Boundaries,* 72.

2. U2, "Original of the Species," How to Dismantle an Atomic Bomb, copyright © 2004, Interscope Records.

## Chapter 11: Get to Know Your Enemy

1. Martha Stout, *The Sociopath Next Door: The Ruthless Versus the Rest of Us* (New York: Three Rivers, 2006), 6.

2. M. E. Thomas, "Confessions of a Sociopath," *Psychology Today,* May/June 2013, www.psychologytoday.com/articles/201305 /confessions-sociopath?collection=122715.

3. The perpetrator and the child can be either male or female, but for the sake of clarity I have labeled the perpetrator as male and the victim as female in this example.

4. M. E. Thomas, *Confessions of a Sociopath: A Life Spent Hiding in Plain Sight* (New York: Crown, 2013), 33.

5. For legal reasons, I cannot reveal the exact relationship or identity of this person.

6. Stout, *The Sociopath Next Door,* 50.

7. Stout, *The Sociopath Next Door,* 108.

## Chapter 12: Jesus Is the Perfect Model for Love

1. *Webster's Dictionary, New Edition* (New York: Pyramid Communications, 1972), s.v. "redemption."

2. J. Lee Grady, *Fearless Daughters of the Bible: What You Can Learn from 22 Women Who Challenged Tradition, Fought I njustice and Dared to Lead* (Grand Rapids: Chosen Books, 2012), 178–79.

## Chapter 13: Your Legacy

1. Henry Cloud, *Integrity: The Courage To Meet the Demands of Reality* (New York: HarperCollins, 2006), 41.

2. Brené Brown, "The Power of Vulnerability," www.ted.com/talks /brene_brown_on_vulnerability?language=en.

3. Summarized from Daniel Amen, MD, *Unleashing the Power of the Female Brain* (New York: Harmony, 2013), 41.

4. M. G. Keefe, *365 Days of Happiness: Inspirational Quotes for Everyone* (Los Gatos, CA: Hot Tropica Books, 2013), 48.

5. Allender, *The Wounded Heart*, 87.

6. Allender, *The Wounded Heart*, 89.

7. Bonnie Harris, *Confident Parents, Remarkable Kids* (Avon, MA: Adams Media, 2008), 31–32.

8. Milan Yerkovich and Kay Yerkovich, *How We Love Workbook* (Colorado Springs: WaterBrook Press, 2006), 78.

9. Strong's Concordance 7965, quoted from "Meaning of the Word 'Shalom,'" *The Refiner's Fire,* www.therefinersfire.org/meaning_ of_shalom.htm.

## Chapter 14: Help for Those Who Help the Overcomers

1. Marshall P. Duke, "The Stories That Bind Us: What Are the Twenty Questions?," *Huffington Post,* March 23, 2013, www.huffingtonpost .com/marshall-p-duke/the-stories-that-bind-us_b_2918975.html.

2. Boz Tchividjian, "Evangelical Christians Release Historic Statement Regarding Sexual Abuse in the Church," American Association of Christian Counselors, July 17, 2013, www.aacc.net/2013/07/17 /evangelical-christians-release-historic-statement-regarding -sexual-abuse-in-the-church/.

3. Diane Langberg, *On the Threshold of Hope: Opening the Door to Healing for Survivors of Sexual Abuse* (Carol Stream, IL: Tyndale House, 1999), 198–99.

## Chapter 15: Fighting Alongside the Princess Warrior

1. Allender, *The Wounded Heart,* 14.

2. *Webster's Dictionary,* s.v. "compassion."

## Appendix A: You Are Far from Alone

1. "Statistics," Rape, Abuse, and Incest National Network, www.rainn .org/statistics.

2. Callie Marie Rennison, "Rape and Sexual Assault: Reporting to Police and Medical Attention, 1992–2000" August 2002. Retrieved from the US Department of Justice, Office of Justice Programs, Bureau of Justice Statistics, http://bjs.ojp.usdoj.gov/content/pub/pdf /rsarp00.pdf.

3. M. Heenan and S. Murray, "Study of reported rapes in Victoria 2000–2003": Summary research report. State of Victoria (Australia),

Department of Human Services (2006), www.dhs.vic.gov.au/_data
/assets/pdf_file/0004/644152/StudyofReportedRapes.pdf. K. A.
Lonsway, J. Archambault, and D. Lisak, "False reports: Moving
beyond the issue to successfully investigate and prosecute non-stranger
sexual assault." The Voice, 3, no. 1, 1–11, 2009. Retrieved from the
National District Attorneys Association: www.ndaa.org/pdf/the
_voice_vol_3_no_1_2009.pdf. D. Lisak, L. Gardinier, S. C. Nicksa,
and A. M. Cote, "False Allegations of Sexual Assault: An Analysis of
Ten Years of Reported Cases," Violence Against Women 16, no. 12,
1318–34, 2010. www.icdv.idaho.gov/conference/handouts/False
-Allegations.pdf

4. Kathleen C. Basile, abstract of "Prevalence of Wife Rape and Other
   Intimate Partner Sexual Coercion in a Nationally Representative
   Sample of Women," Violence and Victims 17, no. 5 (October 2002):
   511–24, www.ncbi.nlm.nih.gov/pubmed/12477095.

5. Diana E. H. Russell, abstract of Rape in Marriage, rev. ed. (Bloom-
   ington, IN: Indiana University Press, 1990), www.dianarussell.com
   /books.html.

6. Kathleen C. Basile, 2002, cited in the presentation offered by Merve
   Davies, PhD and Dominique Simons, PhD, ATSA (Association for
   the Treatment of Sexual Abusers) Conference 2009.

7. Park, "WHO: 1 in 3 Women."

8. Louise McOrmono-Plummer, 2004, cited in the presentation offered
   by Merve Davies, PhD and Dominique Simons, PhD, ATSA Conference 2009.

9. Boz Tchividjian, "Worship and Children—The Eternal Connection,"
   GRACE: Godly Response to Abuse in the Christian Environment,

http://static1.squarespace.com/static/54596334e4b0780b44555981
/t/54710507e4b022d59e033565/1416692999505/Worship-and
-Children1.pdf.

10. Personal conversation with the author.

## Appendix B: Posttraumatic Stress Disorder, the Wounded Brain

1. *Diagnostic and Statistical Manual,* Text Revision (Washington DC: American Psychiatric Association, June 2000), 476, 468.

2. Sethanne Howard and Mark W. Crandall, "Post Traumatic Stress Disorder: What Happens in the Brain?" *Journal of the Washington Academy of Sciences* 93, no. 3 (Fall 2007): 14, www.washacadsci .org/Journal/Journalarticles/V.93-3-Post%20Traumatic%20Stress %20Disorder.%20Sethanne%20Howard%20and%20Mark%20 Crandalll.pdf.